Marketing in Food, Hospitality, Tourism and Events

A Critical Approach

Richard Tresidder and Craig Hirst

 **Goodfellow Publishers Ltd**

(G) Published by Goodfellow Publishers Limited,
Woodeaton, Oxford, OX3 9TJ

http://www.goodfellowpublishers.com

British Library Cataloguing in Publication Data: a catalogue record for this title is available from the British Library.

Library of Congress Catalog Card Number: on file.

ISBN: 978-1-906884-22-2

Design and typesetting by P.K. McBride, www.macbride.org.uk

Cover design by Cylinder, www.cylindermedia.com

Printed by Marston Book Services, www.marston.co.uk

Contents

About the authors

Richard Tresidder is Senior Lecturer in Hospitality Marketing at the Sheffield Business School, Sheffield Hallam University. He holds a doctorate in the semiotics of tourism and is particularly interested in the socio-anthropology of tourism, hospitality, events and food and how these experiences are represented in marketing texts.

Craig Hirst is a Senior Lecturer in Food Marketing at the Sheffield Business School, Sheffield Hallam University. He presently leads the school's MSc Food Consumer Marketing and Product Development. Craig has an interest in the cultural dynamics of the marketplace and its influence upon food marketing practice and consumer behaviour. His interest spans to the tourism, hospitality and event sectors.

Acknowledgements

I would like to thank Emmie for all support and understanding during the production of this book. I would also like to thank our colleagues at the Sheffield Business School for providing us with the space and understanding to produce this piece of work.

RT

I would like to thank Faye and Ralph for their generosity in allowing the time and space to complete this book. Their support and patience has been immeasurable. We will be having a new member joining our family shortly and I dedicate this piece to all of you. I also express gratitude to all the students and colleagues who have helped the development of ideas that feature in this book, thanks for letting me trial them on you. Finally to my parents and Mick and Lynn for being so supportive and taking away some of the pressures that are so integral to this process. Thanks to you all.

CH

Additionally we would like to thank Tim and Sally at Goodfellow Publishers for their patience and support from the submission of the initial proposal to the full manuscript.

 # Introduction

■ Why this book is needed

This book was motivated by a lecture series presented by the two authors at the Sheffield Business School. The module aimed to provide a critical framework for students to apply their previous marketing knowledge to the marketing of tourism, hospitality, events and food (THEF). During this time, although there was a large body of critical and conceptual marketing literature being produced within the sector, there was not a definitive text that reflected these debates and brought together a critical framework in which to surround the marketing of THEF experiences that could be recommended to students. As a result, it was decided that this book should be written.

The study of tourism, hospitality, events and food has a long tradition of academic development that has mixed management concepts and a social science based discourse. This multidisciplinary approach is reflected in the majority of THEF university courses and has given rise to many special interest groups that have forwarded knowledge in the subject area. This has created a critical approach to the contemporary study and analysis of THEF. However, the theoretical development of marketing in the subject area has largely developed around marketing practice and general marketing concepts and theory rather than developing a critical understanding of the marketing process within these sectors specifically. THEF form both a significant element of the service economy and a critically important role in the lives of consumers.

Consumers use tourism, hospitality, events and food as markers of their lives, they save to escape for a couple of weeks and justify working hard to engage in what is fundamentally a significant aspect of their lives. While we hope to stimulate the debates that surround marketing in our sector, the ideas in this publication are not to be considered a replacement; therefore this work should be seen and treated as a complementary text that is used alongside more management orientated texts. The purpose of this book is to provide a critical insight into many of the process that inform elements of marketing such as segmentation, targeting and positioning and specifically the role of marketing in creating meaning and value.

This book adopts a critical approach to marketing that it draws its inspiration not just from the academic debates that surround and inform contemporary marketing practices, but also from the areas of sociology, anthropology, cultural studies, tourism, events and hospitality studies, the theory of food, critical marketing and social theory. This multidisciplinary approach enables the marketer to adopt a holistic approach that links together business studies and the social sciences, the result is to create an inclusive, creative and rigorous approach to marketing. The ability to understand the world we live in respect of the wants, needs, desires and aspirations of the consumer, and their relationship, to tourism, hospitality, events and food, and the elements is fundamental to being a successful practitioner in these sectors. In conclusion, the adoption of a critical approach to marketing provides the marketer with a set of theoretical and conceptual tools that will enhance practice and effectiveness.

The dominant approach to marketing that you see duplicated in nearly all generic marketing texts and marketing programmes serves to replicate the marketing paradigm that is embedded in notions of economic and psychological exchange. There is much value in these texts and this general approach as they advance our understanding of developments in marketing practice and provide industry-relevant data and case studies. There are a few exceptions to this exchange approach, notably the work of consumer culture theory (CCT) researchers who collectively acknowledge that marketing is located within a broader framework of practices that serve (to reproduce) the marketplace. This book aligns with this philosophy and many of the themes identified by the CCT tradition are explored in this book. The benefits of adopting a more socially and culturally aware approach enables the marketer to understand how culture shapes marketplace trends, consumer behaviours and the practice of the market and marketer themselves. This approach also liberates the consumer from being identified as merely a target to be acted upon.

There are certain themes that run throughout the book that inform the agenda for the critical marketing of THEF, these include:

■ Power

■ Culture

■ Motivations

■ Marketplace meanings and value(s)

■ Marketplace resources and practices

■ Ethics and morality

■ How to use this book

This book provides a critical analysis of the marketing process and as such should be used alongside more traditionally orientated marketing books. The theory developed in this publication does not supersede the work of authors such as Kotler, Solomon or Vargo and Lusch, rather it complements it by offering an alternative method of greater understanding of the marketing process. Additionally, the book provides an insight into the particular nature of the marketing of tourism, hospitality, events and food in the form of experiences marketing. This is of particular importance, as the nature of the subject matter is extraordinarily rich in social, cultural and individual significance. In order to effectively market, or promote such experiences it is important to understand how this significance is embedded in contemporary consumer society. This book provides an introduction to critical marketing within the sector and the structure and content of the chapters will take you through an academic journey that builds towards a manifesto for the effective marketing of tourism, hospitality, events and food in Chapter 10.

■ Structure and outline of chapters

Chapter 2, *Locating the Experience in Experience Marketing*, explores how experiences marketing must differ from the norm. It achieves this by examining how tourism, events, hospitality and food fulfils such a significant role in contemporary society, culture and the economy generally. This chapter explores the sociological and cultural foundations of the experiences provided by these sectors, and how consumers relate to, and engage them as part of their everyday lived experience. As such, this section provides the foundations for the remainder of the book. Concepts that are central to THEF experiences are defined and described that feature within each of the subsequent chapters. Just as tourism, hospitality, events and food reflect social and cultural movements, so should its marketing.

Chapter 3, *Perspectives of Marketing*, locates the concept of experiences marketing within current mainstream marketing debates. Although this book offers an alternative or complement to contemporary marketing practices it is important to recognise that much of the literature has been motivated or has emerged from these central and traditional marketing debates. Numerous perspectives of marketing exist. These together frame the way in which we think about the nature of marketing and ultimately provide the logic and frameworks that govern practice. As such, this chapter explores these perspectives in order to enable the reader to integrate the alternative theoretical debates offered in other chapters into their own approach. These in order of where they feature include (1) the exchange perspective, (2) marketing as service and interaction, and (3) marketing a cultural process and practice.

Chapter 4, *Consumption Resources and THEF Experiences*, investigates notions of consumption and consumers. It is important that we understand what is meant by consumption and how we locate the consumer within the consumption process. The THEF sectors, utilise a complex set of codes, images and material practices to stage a very particular product or experience. Importantly the consumption of tourism, hospitality, events and even food differs from other products, by the fact that we are dealing with experiences rather than tangible goods such as a car. This chapter helps to locate what is consumed and how this happens. Additionally this chapter locates the consumer by challenging traditional notions of market segmentation by offering a culturally orientated alternative.

Chapter 5, *Consumption and the Consumer*, acknowledges both the service-dominant and cultural perspectives of marketing, which together recognise that marketplace meanings, value(s) and experiences are created through the consumption process. This deviates from the dominant view that expresses that value and meaning is exchanged through transactions, and at the point and moment of purchase. Accordingly, the focus of understanding consumers from the point of being discrete market segments that display a set of characteristics which together will constitute their consumption preferences and patterns switches to one in which we analyse the consumer resources that are brought to bare and integrated with marketplace resources in the creation and production of valuable and meaningful THEF experiences. This is essential knowledge in the THEF sectors where consumers are seen to engage in protracted and complex interactions and relationships with the marketplace.

Chapter 6, *Habitus, Distinction, Identity and Cultural Capital*, examines how consumption patterns are used by consumers to define their position within society. The choices of experiences are central to this process, as the food we eat, the destinations we visit, the events we attend and how we consume them become social markers of who we are or want to be. The significance of this is manifold as our tastes and consumption practices locate us within consumption groups or tribes, and conversely exclude us from others. Understanding group membership and dynamics provide an alternative means of segmenting or targeting potential customers, thereby offering a more nuanced approach to this critical marketing function. This complements more traditional approaches such as demographic, socio-economic and psychographic traditions.

Chapter 7, *Interpreting Marketing*, charts how individuals interpret and make sense of marketing. It recognises how the life-world and personal biographies of individual consumers inform how they find meaning within marketing, experiences and consumption. By understanding how consumers approach the interpretation process, it enables marketers to shape and construct marketing strategies more efficiently and effectively.

Chapter 8, *The Semiotics of Experience*, explores how the marketing of tourism, hospitality, events and food rests upon a number of signs, images and themes to convey and produce the experience to the consumer. This process creates a language of experience that can be defined as a semiotic convention or approach. By examining various aspects of marketing it is possible to identify a semiotic language that is utilised by marketers and is read and understood by the consumer. Semiotics is simply the study of signs, images and the significance of where the marketing communication is placed and outlines how the consumer reads them. Therefore, brochures, flyers, television adverts and websites etc. use various conventions that are encoded with meanings and messages which creates a desire within the individual for that particular event or experience. As marketers it is important that we understand this semiotic language and semiotics generally, as it means that we can tailor and construct a practice of marketing that the consumer understands, creates relationships, and stimulates desire for the product or experience. The chapter closes with an examination of the power implications of meaning based approaches to marketing practice.

Chapter 9, *Ethics, Sustainability and the Green Consumer*, analyses how the politics of sustainability and the green agenda influence and impact on the marketing of THEF. There is a growing acknowledgment within THEF marketing that it is mutually beneficial to work towards a sustainable agenda. The ethics of the production, dissemination and consumption of THEF experiences is becoming increasingly questioned across a number of dimensions. These include concerns about cultural social and environmental sustainability. There is a long traditional of sustainable tourism experiences that range from trekking in undeveloped areas to visiting Center Parcs, while food production has developed clear links with the 'Fairtrade', organic and slow food movements. Organisations such as Marriott Hotels have invested heavily in their green credentials and large events such as Glastonbury Music Festival have their foundations in raising money for charities. As such the notion of sustainability has become one of the central themes to experiences marketing and has seen the emergence of the green consumer. The theme of sustainability within experiences marketing can be seen to fulfil a number of objectives that can be broadly divided into two elements. The first is where sustainability is used as a means of product differentiation, adds to the brand value, reinforces the credentials of the organisation, impacts on buyer choice, in other words it adds an economic value to the company's or organisation's product. The second element is the impact the notion of sustainability has on the consumer's perception of products, how it makes us feel and ultimately how it makes us behave. It is the contention of this book that THEF marketing should be an inclusive practice that takes consideration of a broad range of stakeholder interests.

In summarising this publication, Chapter 10, *Conclusion: a manifesto for critical marketing in THEF*, presents a manifesto for the development of a critical approach to the marketing of tourism, hospitality, events and food. The approach offers an inclusive and holistic method to contemporary marketing practice within the field of experiences marketing.

■ Conclusion

Although this book is broken into chapters and many of the debates are intertwined with each other, the book has been constructed to enable the reader to 'dip their toes' into the specific subject themes developed within the chapter. The book if you read it in its entirety will take you on a journey that will introduce the major critical themes that have emerged within the field of marketing. Although, this work presents an approach that is often critical of traditional approaches, it must be reiterated that these remain and will always remain the cornerstone of management practice. Although this may be the case it is important that as students, academics and practitioners that we question and analyse or approaches, assumptions and practices.

Putting the Experiences in Experiences Marketing

■ **Introduction**

In order to understand how experiences marketing needs to differ from other forms of marketing, we first need to identify why THEF plays such a significant role in contemporary society and so, as a consequence, that its marketing requires special attention. Just as THEF reflect social and cultural movements, so does its marketing. As the western world has moved from what may be defined as the era of modernity into the era of post-industrialisation/modernity, this shift has been accompanied by certain social, cultural and economic traits that have resulted in a restructuring of society (Harvey 1989; Lash and Urry 1994). It is argued that this has led to a period of 'social (dis)-organization' (Franklin and Crang 2001:7). This 'social (dis)-organization' can be seen to be the result of an alleged fragmentation of society and culture (Harvey 1989). We now live in a society that is dominated by the media, traditional communities have broken up, trends are fleeting, our lives change very quickly. This has resulted in a feeling of uncertainty and as a result of this uncertainty we have turned to activities that provide comfort and meaning, contemporary experiences marketing frames these activities within the marketing language and processes of food, tourism, hospitality and food.

Additionally experiences marketing reflects the social and cultural movements that circulate contemporary society and draw on discourses, rituals and trends to create a complex form of marketing practice that offers the entry into a dreamscape in which emotions and the needs of the consumer are met by utilising a range of strategies, conventions and representations that differentiates experiences marketing from other forms of marketing. Before the significance and meaning of experiences marketing can be charted, it is important to identify themes have emerged from the shift to the post-industrial to the modern era, as experiences marketing can be perceived as both the result of these themes and as a reaction to them. For authors such as Eco (1995) and Foucault (1987) the contemporary world is dominated by signs, the result of which is that the individual's social and cultural location is governed by 'simulational' (Foucault 1987) and 'hyperreal' (Eco 1995) relations. As Baudrillard asserts:

> The era of simulation is everywhere initiated by the inter-changeability of previously contradictory and dialectical terms ... the inter-changeability of the beautiful and the ugly in fashion; of the right and the left in politics; of the true and false in every media message; of the useful and useless at the level of objects; and of nature and culture at every level of meaning. All the great humanist criteria of value, all the values of a civilisation of moral, civic and practical judgement, vanish in our system of images and signs. Everything becomes undecidable.

(1993: 128)

The result of this for the individual is that the relationship between the signified and signifier becomes blurred, for example, as a reaction to the current economic downturn food retailers have introduced basic ranges that include smoked salmon, extra virgin olive oil etc. thus blurring the boundaries between categories of food. The Venetian Hotel in Las Vegas offers you the opportunity to sit down outside the Coliseum drinking a cappuccino while the Roman sunset romantically sets every twenty minutes. This version of the world becomes central to the discourse that creates the foundations of experiences marketing.

The continued globalisation and preoccupation with signs, brands and the media within contemporary society has led to a type of spatial dislocation. For Jameson:

> this latest mutation in space – post-modern hyperspace – has finally succeeded in transcending the capacities of the individual human body to locate itself, to organise its immediate surroundings perceptually, and cognitively to map its position in a mappable external world.

> (1991: 44)

According to Jameson people no longer know where they are, they are lost both socially and spatially in the processes of the de-differentiation of culture and society. Experiences marketing is a direct result of this de-differentiation, as it plays representations of time, place, emotions, relationships, destinations and experiences by creating a dreamscape in which the consumer can escape everyday life. Mike Featherstone comments that:

> If we examine the definitions of postmodernism we find an emphasis on the effacement of the boundary between art and everyday life, the collapse of the distinction between high art and mass/popular culture, a general stylistic promiscuity and playful mixing of codes.

> (1991: 65)

The consequence of this de-differentiation is a breakdown in the distinctiveness of each area of social and cultural activity, each area implodes into one another bringing at every opportunity, spectacle or play. The impact of this on the consumer is that the relationship between the world represented in experiences marketing and the real world become blurred and often emptied of signs of the modern such as cars or telegraph poles. This emptying of markers of development, people or technology has the effect of providing the consumer greater freedom to find individual meaning within the interpretation process. This is achieved in experiences marketing by utilising a collage of words and images that creates a very specific language of experiences (This will be further discussed in Chapter 8).

The impact of collage and the blurring of boundaries in cultural production, media and THEF marketing directly influences the individual's personality and their relationship to marketing communications by shifting reference points. For example, there has been a trend for fusion food whereby food styles and traditions become blurred creating a distinctive gastronomic style. However food reflects both culture and geography, its grounding means something to people, fusion food no longer relates food to geography, but it does relate to a more global definition of culture. Marketers, designers and editors draw from global cultures creating global trends, however this makes it difficult for us to think about how the things we buy, eat or drink link us to notions of home. For Jameson (1985) this creates a form of schizophrenia as we draw from a range of influences, cultures and style that do not link together and we lose links to foundations that defined our culture and identity. Harvey states:

> If personal identity is forged through 'a certain temporal unification of the past and future with the present before me,' and if sentences move through the same trajectory, then an inability to unify past, present, and future in the sentence betokens a similar inability to 'unify the past, present and future of our own biographical experience...'

> (1995: 53)

What this means for experience marketing is that the use of timeless images removes an element of meaning or signposting of experience, so that the individual consumer will be able to mediate their own THEF experiences, values and world view to create their own understanding or interpretation of the represented experience (see Chapter 7). In practice this creates a problem for the marketer, as they have to accept that, the marketing process will be understood in multiple ways by consumers, as the above process frees or separates them from their established cultural foundations. For example, when we visit an iconic destination such as the London Eye, we arrive with a set of temporal knowledges that draw from sources such as films, television, news, advertisements, literature and personal experiences. As a consequence, our understanding is formed by a collage of historical and cultural influences.

Contemporary marketing practice's preoccupation with the signifier (the image) rather than the signified (meaning) and with surface rather than roots, reduces marketing to 'a series of pure and unrelated presents in time' (Jameson 1985). As such, postmodernism creates a form of social and cultural fragmentation (Jameson 1984) that leads to a lack of coherence within the production of signs and images and as such it impacts upon the individual's perception of the world by dislocating reference points. Experiences marketing is located within two interrelated debates; firstly, that the signs and images contained within the advert reflect the postmodern traits of de-differentiation etc. and secondly, that the consumer may find some sense of comfort or belonging within experience marketing by entering into the dreamscapes created within campaigns.

The previous sections of this chapter are important in understanding the significance of experiences marketing as it is argued that the shift to a post-industrialisation has led to consumers feelings of 'rootless' (Lane and Waitt 2001) and 'alienated' (Gabriel 1993) and created new wants and desires (to have the ideal body, partner, car, holiday meal etc.), that can never be achieved (Rojek 1995), as trends are constantly changed and reconstructed by the media. It is within this environment that the marketing and consumption of THEF plays a stabilising role for both society and the consumer. Experiences marketing offers what Uzzell (1984) refers to as an 'escape hatch' from the pressures and uncertainty of modern society. This is achieved by experiences marketing drawing from a range of discourses and traditions that enable us to find roots in a rootless society, to escape and make sense of everyday life. Experience marketing creates a time and space that is different from everyday lived experience and is central to the message contained within THEF marketing communications. The first way in which experiences marketing creates escape hatches is to create a notion of time that reflects the entry into the dreamscapes.

■ Experiences marketing and the sacred

The experience marketing utilises a set of conventions and approaches that represents events, tourism, hospitality and food in a particular way that has a heightened significance within the rootlessness of the post-industrial/modern world. Experiences marketing both utilises and creates a discourse of THEF that differentiates representations of time and space by elevating the represented experience to that of the 'extraordinary' and is in direct opposition to everyday reality. This process is best demonstrated in food marketing, for example we see a ready meal being presented in a fine dining or aesthetically constructed frame, which breaks the link between the mundane nature of ready meals and elevating it to the extraordinary or even the sacred (see Tresidder 2010, 2011a). The configuration of time and space utilised within experiences marketing is specific to the promotion of THEF and, experience marketing reinforces the binary relationship between the profane/everyday and the sacred/extraordinary nature of the experience. For example tourist advertisements will often show the tourist at work and then on holiday, the convention will often make work dark and rainy, while holiday is light and sunny. We can understand this differentiation of time and space by developing Durkheim's (1995) conception of the 'sacred and profane' within food, hospitality, events and tourism marketing.

THEF marketing becomes just one of the means by which the consumer frames their experiences of the social, and as such, constitutes an important role in their life. Just as Silverstone (1988) envisages television as a 'ritual frame', a cognitive, imaginative and practical space in which everyone can access the things that mark off the social from the private (Couldry 2001: 158), it can be argued that experiences marketing constructs a ritual frame or lens that is composed with marketing texts. Tourism and events marketing marks the distinction between social experience and ordinary experience, and subsequently what may be termed the sacred and the profane. For Durkheim (1995) the conception of the sacred and profane are socially generated and underline the distinction between social and ordinary experience. While Caillois (1988: 20) meanwhile, recognised that the two worlds of the mutually exclusive domains of the sacred and profane do not mingle in unmediated ways, that is, in the absence of collectively recognised rites of passage and acknowledged risks of admixture (Belk *et al.* 1989). Commenting on Bourdieu's conception of the sacred and profane, Genosko commented that:

> He took great care to outline how the profane needs the sacred, and the regulation, through rites, of the process of consecration in the passage into the sacred from the profane.
>
> (2003: 75)

The sacred or extraordinary status of THEF are reinforced by its social and cultural production and consumption, but also by experiences marketing as signifying something 'extraordinary' or the 'sacred sphere of excess' (Caillois 1988: 282) within campaigns. It is within this discussion, that the sacred and profane is a useful analogy for the distinction between the sacred world of tourism, hospitality, events and food as represented in experiences marketing and the profane world of everyday lived experience (see Sheldrake 2001).

A major theme of experiences marketing is that it is not the everyday (Belk *et al.* 1989), but is a means of escape from our everyday lived experience of working, cooking the daily meal, utilitarian shopping and washing the dishes. By adopting Caillois' view (1998) that the sacred had shifted from celebration at the societal level to 'individualized isolated experiences' (Genosko 2003: 76), whereby the entry into the extraordinary sacred world of experiences marketing becomes an individual quest in which the individual consumer may find meaning and escape in their own lives, the relationship we have to experiences marketing is formed by our personality, as well as are worldview (see Chapter 7). This notion of escape is identified by Berlyn who suggests that human life tries to maintain a preferred level of arousal and seeks: 'artificial sources of stimulation...to make up for the shortcomings of their environment' (1977: 170). The content and structure can be examined against the ordinary workaday life and that attending an event, or family holiday or special meal become the markers of the passage time, making up part of our memories and personal biography.

There is large body of work that identifies how activities such as THEF may be seen to provide a link into societal and cultural functions traditionally provided by religion in terms of celebration, finding yourself or justifying yourself. It is argued that the increasing secularisation of society, has left a vacuum or void in everyday life (York 2001), and rather than working and saving hard and reaping your rewards in the next life you no longer have to wait, you can fill this gap by engaging in the extraordinarily places, spaces and activities offered in experiences marketing. Traditionally religion was perceived as either a system of beliefs which binds people together into social groups (Durkheim 1995) or more importantly, that religion is a set of coherent answers to the human existential dilemmas of birth, sickness and death (Weber 1978). In this sense, religion is the human response to the existential questions of contemporary life. The implications of these approaches, is that food, hospitality, tourism and events provides a release from the pressures of everyday life through creating celebratory frames in which the consumer can make sense of the contemporary world by exploring at the promotional level the significance of experience.

As stated previously, experiences marketing creates a ritual frame, 'a cognitive and practical space' (Couldry 2001: 158) in which the consumer negotiate the 'social', the words, images and structure of experiences marketing creates a marketing language that is embedded in the society or culture that the marketer has targeted. Rituals have to be repetitive, have rules and contain a social element that are understood by society; in short they are a code of behaviour with a sacred element (Stirrat 1984), the consumer understands the significance of food, events, tourism and hospitality and also knows the rules and expected or ritualistic behaviour when engaging in them. Additionally rituals generally exhibit 'effervescence, pleasure, games ... all that recreates the spirit that has been fatigued by the too great slavishness of daily work' (Durkheim 1995:426). What was sacred for Durkheim (1995) was society itself, and this involved the sacralisation of the social where, the object of worship was society itself, as he states 'anything ... can be sacred' (1995:35). We use tourism, events, food and hospitality as a central element in any form of celebration or ritual, whether that is celebrating personal achievements, sporting events, births, deaths and marriages or even saints, and experiences marketing needs to reflect this celebration of society and culture. It achieves this by adopting a number of marketing conventions that are understood by the consumer and in which they find meaning, these conventions will be explored in some depth later in this book.

■ Time and space

The use of time and space in experiences marketing is one of the most widely used and significant conventions, campaigns will clearly structure their advertisements to show the differences between everyday life and the sacred spaces of THEF. For example, everyday food is shown in a setting that is outside the ordinary, the use of black and while shots reinforces the timelessness of tourism while creating individual events that encourage you to escape. Durkheim's view was that the sacred was simply society transposed onto the spiritual level, and the distinction between the sacred and the profane is a universal social fact; 'The sacred and the profane have always and everywhere been conceived by the human mind as two distinct classes' (1995: 38–39). It is this idea that THEF creates different times within communications which underpins the assertion that experiences marketing differs in its significance and structure from other forms of marketing. The sacred does not deny any notion of time, but rather the notion of the sacred as represented within experiences marketing, is conceived as timeless and authentic experiences (authenticity of landscape, people, personal relationships, food, culture and experience) which transport us into a time and space that has become sacred. As Stirrat states:

> To be truly at one with the sacred involves attaining an existence outside time and space, and thus to be truly sacred, religious virtuosi must attempt to live outside society.
>
> (1984: 203)

Experiences marketing provides an opportunity to live outside the time and space of everyday life for a limited period, the signs and images utilised in THEF marketing create an alternative temporal and spatial dimension which becomes central to everyday life as offering a form of escape.

■ Liminality

Experiences advertising and marketing uses a notion of temporal and spatial liminality in which the consumer is released from their normal social constraints, the representations of liminality within the advert 'signposts' (Jenkins 2003) vicarious esoteric or metaphysical consumption of tourism and events. Liminality may be defined as a place or event that is out-of or in-between time,

2

for example we do things on holiday we do not do at home as we are in a time that is different from our everyday life. The liminal space that exists within the marketing communication continuum between transmission of the marketing message and the actual consumption of the product witnesses the blurring of the boundaries between reality and the imagined consumption of the product. This liminal period releases the consumer from the imposed norms of everyday lived experience or the social constraints and implications of over consumption etc. It enables the virtual entrance into a world of hedonism and escape, thus experiences marketing becomes a reflexive, expressive activity in which individuality is reinforced because we are freed from the constraints of social structures. Turner (1973) characterises this temporal and spatial removal from social constraints as 'antistructure', whereby the content of the social relations is no longer normative and hierarchical but egalitarian, this is a process which he hails as 'communitas'. Experiences marketing creates a form of 'communitas' whereby people bridge their social and cultural differences by finding communitas through shared consumption patterns and a process of harmonisation that enables them to escape and find freedom from the constraints of their normal lives. Turner states that this freedom results in a process that he classifies as 'flow' (1977: 48–52) and can be characterised as:

> the non-reflective stage that is characteristic of a person who is engaged in some important activity, in which action and awareness emerge, self awareness gives way to attention focused on a limited field in which the participant is engaged in mastering, a feeling which is a reward in itself, not a means to an external end. While such feelings may characterise those engaged in religious acts, e.g., taking communion, they are also common to leisure occupations, such as hobbies, sex acts, recreation, and games.
>
> (Graburn 1986: 545)

The ritual status of THEF and the search for meaning and experiences through their consumption becomes a contemporary form of pilgrimage. Experiences marketing enables us to travel the world consuming different tastes and experiences without leaving home. THEF becomes celebrated and even worshipped. It is this hedonistic element that becomes central to so many pilgrimages (see Pfaffenberger 1979), that reinforces the significance of experiences marketing. The next two sections will explore how hospitality and food, and events and tourism become elevated to the level of the sacred within experiences marketing.

■ Imagination

This book, particularly in this chapter, explores the experiences that make up our understanding of THEF. It draws upon discourses and themes that include escape, authenticity, creativity, aesthetics, ambience, stimulation, fun, adventure, excitement. It is interesting to examine how experiences marketing draws upon these themes and creates a stimulational world and space that sparks the imagination. For Schau (2000: 50), imagination is 'a fundamental everyday intellectual practice'. Moreover, it is integral to both consumption practices and people's quotidian experiences in consumer society. While it is of the mind, imagination is something that is grounded in sensation and experience. That is to say, the possibilities of what can be imagined are contained and structured by what has previously been perceived by the senses. This being the case however, imagination is both reproductive and productive (Kant 1965 in Schau 2000). Through synthesising and reconfiguring data and information that is stored in memory one can at once create new possibilities, enter fantasy worlds, anticipate or dream of what is to come, and recreate the past. Accordingly, it is possible to re-imagine events, holidays, meals, encounters, selves and relationships that cognitively approximate to direct experience, but also through imagination, one can construct new stories of what could have been, or who one was, or what may be yet to come. It is also possible though imagination for consumers to enter past worlds and events without having directly experienced them.

Through imagination one can transcend one's own physically bounded biological, temporal and spatial context or in other words, everyday lived experience. In this respect, imagination is integral to consumption and consumer experience as it is a resource of significant value and variability. This variability is illustrated by Jenkins (2011) who offers a taxonomy of imagination and its relation to, and role in consumption that encompasses six categorical concepts and variables. These are:

1 Fanciful

2 Aspirational

3 Anticipatory

4 Nostalgic

5 Guided

6 Prospective

Jenkin's taxonomy is differentiated across a spectrum or continuum of imaginations, that commence with those that are purely fantastical and idyllic, and which are directed towards the escape from material reality, to those that orientated towards present reality and current concerns. That is to say, that imagination is deployed and directed towards 'planning, organising and decision making', resolving problems, and managing and setting expectations (Jenkins, 2011: 208). This element of imagination directly links to the purchasing and consumption of THEF experiences, as we all plan, dream and overcome problems in achieving them, it is in fact one of the enjoyable elements that establish THEF as a significant activity. To elaborate on Jenkin's analysis of imagination we will outline three of these conceptual categories in more detail below.

■ Fanciful imagination

The function of fanciful imagination is to escape mundane or profane experiences or to compensate for felt dissatisfaction. It is fanciful in the sense that the imaginations are not perceived to be manifestly or materially possible. This could be because a consumer may not presently have, or anticipate having the material resources needed to realise a fantasy. Likewise they may not have the skills or physical capability. In other cases the world a consumer constructs may not even exist. It could be an imagined utopia for example. In many cases fanciful imagining is more pleasurable than any alternative or possible material reality, as a hyper-real world can be constructed in the mind that draws from a smorgasbord of hedonic and affective realms of experience that are tied together and sequenced in seemingly impossible ways. Despite this, 'real' consumption and consumer contexts are often central to the experience in two principal ways.

First one could be fantasising about an immersive multi-sensory experience of eating an amazing meal or vicariously consuming the risk and heightened excitement of hurtling down a snow-covered mountain strapped to a snowboard. That is you are imaging yourself engaging in a real act of consumption, whereby a consumer good or practice is in the foreground.

Second, consumer products and experiences could be in the background yet still essential to a particular episode of fantasy. For example one could be imagining the early developmental stages of a romantic relationship. This peak emotional experience could be being played out on a deserted exotic beach on an island in the Indian Ocean or in the midst of a swaying crowd at a rock festival. In this respect while fantastical this mode of imagination is often framed by our 'hopes, dreams and aspirations' (Jenkins 2011: 203).

■ Nostalgic imagination

Nostalgia is experienced through mentally revisiting and recollecting the past and is clearly linked to the debates surrounding authenticity and is a recurrent theme in THEF marketing. Statements about authenticity, organic, hand-made or real become a central discourse in experiences marketing, as it offers an entry into a perceived better time and space. Nostalgia is mostly bound up in material reality, as more often than not it focuses on actual events and an individual's past experiences. In this sense the degree to which one is required to engage in abstract thought is limited, however, one may be drawn deeply into nostalgia focusing greatly on the material, relational, symbolic, and affective details of past events and outcomes, but also in some cases, on the emotions and thoughts presently felt. In this sense, nostalgia can be both a recounting or reflexive activity, reminiscent of critical reflection. In terms of affect it can be bitter-sweet. Not only is a consumer disposed to yearning for perceived better times, or to relive or (re)construct 'the good old days' – in both mind or matter, but they may also be experiencing a protracted or recurring mourning for love ones lost, lost irreplaceable possessions (e.g. Grayson and Schulman 2000), or places, identities, and experiences left behind. Nostalgia, can also be prone to bias and selective recollection, whereby things like emotional peaks or troughs may obfuscate other aspects and realms of experience of the time under review. Accordingly the nostalgic imagination is deployed for multiple aims and functions.

Like fanciful imagination it can be employed to escape everyday reality and situations. Daydreams in these instances will correspond with historical accounts and significant moments and experiences of one's life. These could be related to the immediate past but also the distant. Sat at one's desk, a consumer could drift away into pleasurable thoughts of holidays taken or events that unfolded at a family member's wedding, so, similar to fanciful imagination, products can take a leading role or be present in the background of nostalgic imaginings. In other cases however they are expansive and take in the broad range of sites, sounds, interpersonal interactions, and emotions of that time. The opening verse of Rod McKuen's (1967), poem 'The Gypsy Camp', which was later sampled by A Man Called Adam, is a good example of fanciful imagination:

> I put a seashell to my ear and it all comes back; the yellow sun... the Mediterranean blue, the sky, the children running on the beach that day, the Kildare birds marching in formation down to the sea, and back – when my memory wanders, as it does when bad things happen, I put a seashell to my ear and it all comes back; that day... you

The nostalgic memory also plays a role in present and future consumption. Consumers use nostalgia as a resource to inform their consumer choices and practices, this is in the sense that a consumers' history becomes an itinerary for selection, but also something to be re-experienced.

The motive of recreating the past in the present or alternatively avoiding the present through re-staging the past is a widely acknowledged consumer goal and marketing trend and is heavily utilised within the THEF sector to create experiences. In this respect, it is theorised as having a number of antecedents. Holbrook (1993) for example identifies life-cycle effects. Nostalgia in this case can be related to developmental cycles and specifically adolescence which appear to be a consumer's formative years. These years are instrumental. During this period, attitudes, values, preferences and tastes are developed that continue into later life. Concomitant to this, the urge to re-experience these important times swells inside as a consumer ages. Holbrook goes on to quote Davis:

> ...in Western society it is adolescence, and for the privileged classes early adulthood as well, that affords nostalgia its most sumptuous banquets.

> (1979: 57)

and that

> ...the tides of nostalgia which ... wash over middle-aged persons typically carry them back to the songs, films, styles, and fads of their late teens.

> (1979:60)

2

There is however an interesting twist to the relationship with THEF consumption. Rather than nostalgia being the route to consumption it is consumption that provides the link to nostalgia. In these cases products and experiences are sought to evoke memories of these people and the pleasurable moments shared with them. In this way the experience of re-consuming acts in a similar way to a memento or souvenir. Consider this extract of an interview with an 80-year-old female visitor of Blists Hill Victorian Town living museum from Gouldings' (2001: 577) research:

> ...it's only when you come to a place like this it makes you realize the sort of things you miss. I mean it takes you back. I've lost most of my family, my husband's dead and so are a lot of my friends, the ones I've known for years. So when you see things you remember it brings back happy memories. . .

Similarly Russell and Levy (2012) suggest that the urge to re-consume past experiences, to revisit places where couples met or honeymooned by those who have lost loved ones, is not just about attempts at recreating, revisiting, or remembering the past, but is also a strategy that enables the individual to be forward looking and future orientated. This progressive re-consumption is based upon attempts and motivations to extract new experiences from returning to old places, activities and products. In these cases, there is no desire to return to the past per se, what is wanted is something new; a different encounter. Here Russell and Levy (2012) draw upon informant interviews with widowers to explain how the motivation to re-visit the places they had been with their partners. These visits were not rooted in pleasurable attempts at recreation and re-staging of what had been, rather they were about moving forward, they were therapeutic experience. This may also explain the motivations for engaging in dark tourism or visiting battlefields.

> Nelson, now a widower, chose to re-visit Florence and Siena, towns he had visited forty years prior, with his wife and two young children. Revisiting the sites, hotels and restaurants... was 'a kind of pilgrimage, a sentimental journey' that allowed him to 'sadly mourn the loss [of his wife and son], missing them more vividly' but it was mostly a conscious attempt 'to reconcile myself to this time of my life'.
>
> (Russell and Levy 2012: 136)

Progressive re-consumption therefore is a practice that is:

> open to the possibility of change and motivated by the desire to affirm, confirm, or dis-confirm an impression left by previous experiences.
>
> (ibid.: 138)

The consumer in this case may attempt to acknowledge that they are a now a different person to the one that came before and therefore expect to find new things and meanings in an old experience. Consumption in this respect is a rite of passage and transitionary; they seek a new identity or to progressively move away from an old one.

In a similar manner to the above, Brown *et al.* (2003) develop Davies's (1979) work whereby they acknowledge the role of epochal shifts and fractures in society and culture as motivating consumer behaviour. Where terrorist events or natural, cultural or economic disasters pose a significant threat and risk to existential security, and threaten individual and collective identity or families or work there is a propensity to seek security in the past. Consumers attempt this through consuming brands and THEF products with heritage and history that are simultaneously linked to former selves, communal reference points, and perceptions of more secure, communal, and innocuous times. This accounts for the rise in the number of heritage centres, historical re-enactments and claims that food is authentic or 'just like mamma makes' and the continual draw of country houses and television programmes like *Downton Abbey*. In these cases, in contrast to present reality, consumers are moved to romanticise the past and construct it in idealistic, authentic and utopian terms (Goulding 2001). In this context some authors claim that the past has become sacralised, in making this argument Brown *et al.* (2003) cite the great depression of the 1930s, the turmoil of the 1960s, the implosion of communism and subsequent rebalancing of the world order as key transformational events and examples that share this relationship. Each of these periods it is maintained, had a subsequent corresponding period of retrospection, nostalgia and revival. Accordingly, on a par with this reasoning, a nostalgic resurgence and boom should be presently under way given the ongoing economic malaise stemming from the 2008 credit crunch and subsequent recession and predicted return to recession. Indeed we do not need to look far for sector examples, in events we have school and university reunions, the revival of Pop and Indie bands, like Take That, the Stone Roses, and the Happy Mondays who in re-forming are embarking on sell-out and record-breaking tours. For food we have the return of the Wispa bar and the revival of antiquated sweet shops that both physically resemble a bygone age and sell classics like aniseed balls and rhubarb and custard boiled sweets. Hospitality, has witnessed the restaurants which are mining history and bringing back updated versions of classics menu items such as the ubiquitous prawn cocktail and scampi. Equally we have full concepts like 1950s diners, where not only the food is (re)created for the pleasure of diners, but the whole servicescape is theatrically staged and designed including the fashion styles and dress codes of serving staff, décor, music and entertainment. Finally in tourism we have heritage centres, living museums (e.g. Goulding 2001) and re-enactments like Pickering War Weekend. These, while seeking to educate, inspire and remind, offer certain consumers the opportunity to satisfy the nostalgic urge and create opportunities for new and enhanced imaginations.

■ Guided and prospective imagination

We bring together two of Jenkins' (2011) conceptual categories in this final review. Here imagination is predicated and focused on consumption that is either very likely to occur or soon to take place. It is anticipatory in nature and in some cases akin to planning, the imagination here is often deployed creatively. For instance a consumer could be imagining what to cook for friends in an upcoming dinner party. They could equally put their imagination to more immediate use in working out how to make something palatable and fulfilling from food that is left over in the fridge and kitchen cupboards. In a similar vein, a consumer could deploy the imagination in thinking through how to balance scarce material resources with creating a memorable and valuable holiday experience for the family. Relatedly, the imagination is often needed in thinking up exciting activities in which to engage the children whilst on the holiday.

In the examination of an anti-consumption festival, Kozinets (2002a) examines how participants at the Burning Man Festival (www.burningman.com) in their attempt to escape the pressures to consume are expected to draw upon their creative imagination and other resources to produce temporary artworks or engage in practices of radical self-expression and performance art, as well as in radical self-preservation. The latter being integral to the fact that participants must be prepared to survive the harsh environment of the Black Rock Desert of Nevada in which the festival is co-created and performed over the course of a week.

> My sense of Burning Man as entertainment changes a bit as I read the ticket, which states the risks and rules of the event; 'you voluntarily assume the risk of serious injury or death by attending this event. You must bring enough food, water, shelter and first aid to survive one week in a harsh desert environment. Commercial vending, firearms, fireworks, rockets and other explosives prohibited... This is not a con-

2

sumer event. Leave nothing behind when you leave the site. Participants only. No spectators'.

(Kozinets 2002a: 20)

He further states that:

> The most bizarre thing I saw at Burning Man was a man dressed in a three-piece business suit and carrying a briefcase, rushing through the desert one evening. He brushed by a group of us quickly, saying 'excuse me gentlemen,' as if he were late for a meeting. Our group burst out laughing... the source of the humour was the realization that this is a place set far apart from the logics that drive everyday business behaviour in the world of large corporations. Our mock businessman's attire, emoting, utterances and rushing were pure performance art in this desolate and distant location.

(ibid.: 31)

Such experiences guide our relationship to both experiences and their marketing. The themes and discourses that inform the communication of experience within marketing spaces is a metaphysical journey in which we engage all of our senses and most importantly we use our imagination to interpret, locate ourselves within the discourse and most importantly find meaning.

■ Myth and myth making in experiences marketing

It is argued that the notion of tourism (Selwyn 1996; Barthes 1999), hospitality, food (Reed-Danahay 1996) and certain events (see Belk and Costa 1998, below) are underpinned and surrounded by a cultural myth. Experiences marketing draws upon and reinforces these myths through the themes and experiences they communicate to the consumer and for Thompson (2004: 162) '…permeate consumer culture'. The notion of myth elevates the significance of the experience, they are integral to a consumer's knowledge base, myths can essentially be summarised as cultural models and templates through which consumers (and marketers) think, feel and act (Thompson and Arsel, 2004: 632). Drawing on the work of D'Andrade (1990), Miller (1998) and Shore (1996), Thompson and Arsel (2004) go on to show that cultural models are both inter-subjectively shared and also objectified in material reality. That is not only do these templates reside in the minds of consumers they are also inscribed into the artefacts and practices of consumer culture. They are present in brochures, websites, novels, films, TV shows, plays and theatrical performances, brands, advertisements, and the physical design, atmospherics and communicative staging of servicescapes (Arnould *et al.* 1998; Chronis *et al.* 2012). Myths that surround, events, festivals, carnivals, destination, restaurants, certain foods, peoples, landscapes etc. can be conceived as market-ing resources, these may:

1 Be presently integral to the interpretive repertoire of a con-sumer, having been integrated over time through everyday interaction and engagement in the world over their life-course and trajectory.

2 Searched out, located, and assimilated during prepara-tion for, or following a specific mode of consumption. For example in preparing to visit an historic site a consumer may consult historical accounts and records or view serialised TV media to build on their stock of knowledge to enhance their experience. Likewise, on return they may engage in similar activity to augment their knowledge and experience.

3 They could have been 'consumed' during, and through the interaction with the products and services offered by the marketplace itself.

Roland Barthes in his book *The Eiffel Tower and Other Mythologies*, charts how the Eiffel Tower has been defined within literature, the arts and commerce and how as a result of these definitions has comes to represent so much more than just a tourist attraction. The

Eiffel Tower is now used to represent Paris, Romance and even a totem of France. This myth of the tower is then utilised by market-ers to sell and communicate the idea or notion of 'Frenchness' or romance without have to describe or waste time scene setting. This is amazing when you consider that the tower was never meant to be a permanent structure in the first place but was only constructed for the 1889 World's Fair.

Belk (1998) further explores the notion by examining the Mountain Man myth, he charts how this has been perpetuated through historical artefacts, events, festivals and texts that cata-logue and provide accounts that approximate reality, that are rein-forced by folkloric interpretations and works of cultural producers like film-makers, novelists and artists. They cite, 'Gentle Ben, *The Life and Times of Grizzly Adams*, Spirit of the Eagle, *Jeremiah Johnson*, and the Mountain Men Festivals (over 50 held in the USA during 2012) as examples of the latter (Belk and Costa 1998: 221). These he argues, 'implicitly or explicitly' become essential resources and cultural frameworks though which the re-enactments and experi-ences are constructed and mediated by 'modern mountain men (p. 220). They are foundational to what can be experienced.

The mountain man represents a specific example of American social strata in the early to mid-1800s. Belk and Costa's (1998) account suggests that they were around 3000 in number, mostly of white ethnicity who lived and worked around the Rocky Mountains. They scraped out an existence in the dangerous fur trade though trapping beavers and selling and exchanging their pelts. The rendezvous was where they came together to trade. Quoting Cleland (1952: 25), Belk and Costa (1998: 221) describe the rendezvous accordingly:

> Like a medieval fair... it... was a place of buying, selling, haggling, cheating, gambling, fighting, drinking, palavering, racing, shooting and carousing.
>
> (Belk and Costa 1998: 221)

It is this, what the rendezvous participant wishes to recreate. However, in doing this, from Belk and Costa's analysis it is possible to summarise the motive of the modern mountain man has being to temporarily reclaim mastery over one's life, and to transcend the logic that presently prescribes and constrains it. By imitating and (re)creating the lifestyles, practices and behaviours of these idealised people one is able to momentarily reclaim the fundamental essence of human and masculine experience, which are believed to have been lost or diminished amongst the milieu and structuring effects of contemporary post-modern life. The mountain man discourse thus provides a cultural template of the rugged individual and frontier myth that is both idolised and revered in American culture yet simultaneously mourned by a segment of US male consumers (e.g. Holt 2006; Thompson and Holt 2004; Hirschman 2003).

The contemporary rendezvous provides an entry point and liminal time and space in which to (re)experience, (re)create, and celebrate these ideals in contemporary marketing practice, a recent example of this theme is Jean-Claude Van Damme's Coors advert or even the famous/infamous Marlboro Man adverts. Experiences marketing draws heavily from the myths of destinations, events and history etc. It is supported by a myth-making industry (Selywn 1996) that includes television, literature, marketing, culture and even postcards. Again, it is areas of influence such as myth and its significance within consumer society in embedding experience, that separates THEF marketing from other forms of marketing activity.

Myth is located within a historical continuum that permeates the marketing of THEF, the next section charts how the significance of hospitality and food has come to be embedded within contemporary consumption practices.

■ Embedding the practice and myth of hospitality and food

The myth of hospitality and food in experiences marketing are socially and culturally embedded within contemporary life and create consensus constructs. This embedding draws from the historical tradition of hospitality and food (O'Connor 2005; O'Gorman 2007; Claseen 2007). Although the concept of hospitality and food is a significant element of culture, the concept of hospitality and food needs to be contextualised within the time in which it is being judged. For Delind (2007), both the semiotic and physical consumption of gastronomy as contained within experiences marketing provides a refuge from fast food culture and the instantaneous nature of postmodern society. Experiences marketing consumption creates what may be defined as a 'Pleasure Zone' (Fantasia 1995) in which we can escape into utopian food and hospitality space, this space signifies a 'graceful way of living' (Delind 2006: 128), it bounds our past and memory creating a sense of belonging by drawing on the embedded definitions of hospitality and gastronomy. The consumption of hospitality and food is an 'authoritative act' that 'authenticates' (Marshall 2005: 73) our identity and position within the world it acts as a social marker of who we are (Bourdieu 1987; Gvion and Trosler 2008). Experiences marketing draws us into the consumption process and in particular, representations of the restaurant, the hotel or meal make social and cultural life real as experiences marketing is an 'agency of culinary culture, lifestyle and systems' (Gvion and Trosler 2008).

The images used in the experiences marketing create what Johns and Pine (2002: 127) refer to as the 'authentic environments' of hospitality, the images used are empty of humans and modernity, they offer us an empty space in which we can search for the authentic. This is a convention in experiences marketing (see Waitt and Head 2002; Lane and Waitt 2007) and wider cultural debates (Drolet 2004), that not only offers a reflexive space for the individual but reflects the power of the marketer to exclude and include people, culture and places. This notion of emptiness offers a mediation on taste and gastronomy which define the preparation, social character, philosophy, aesthetics of hospitality, food, the table – it identifies food and hospitality as art (Fantasia 1995).

Hospitality and food marketing signposts various escape routes from everyday lived experience that facilitates a notion of escape and the representation of hospitality and food signifies a time and space which is differentiated from everyday lived experience by its 'extraordinariness' and is differentiated from the routine and often un-reflexive consumption of food as merely fuel (Marshall 2005). Consequently, THEF marketing creates a configuration of time and space that elevates the context of the hospitality and food served to that of the extraordinary. For example in a number of adverts from Marks and Spencer, they use a collage of music, settings and dialogue to elevate what is a ready meal to that of fine dining and sophistication (see Tresidder 2011b).

It is within these liminal places or 'pleasure zones' (Fantasia 1995) that we find a release from our normal social constraints and can enter into a state of communitas (Belk *et al.* 1989). The creation of these 'pleasure zones' offers a delineated space that semiotically represents a time, a sophistication in which we may hedonistically explore the experiences of food and hospitality. This liminality and release enables us to explore hospitality and food in terms of senses and the sensual, as an 'intimate frontier' (Dawkins 2009) in which we may locate the body. In other words the embedding of definitions of food and hospitality within experiences marketing enables the individual to explore:

> ...the role of the sensual, the emotional, the expressive, for maintaining layered sets of embodied relationships to food and place.
>
> (Delind 2006: 121)

Often the images used of food in experiences marketing elevate the food and dining experience to the level of food pornography whereby there is a breakdown between sexual and gustatory pleasures and is so removed from real life that it can only be consumed vicariously (Magee 2007). For example the images of finished dishes on restaurant websites, in cookbooks or on television that have been produced by celebrity chefs are so perfect they can never be replicated. This notion is reinforced by Ellis (1980) who states that pornography of representation is anything that is outside the norm. As a consequence, such representations promote a myth of food for Reed-Danahay (1996) the sensual or sexual, reinforcing the images of food in marketing as the binary opposition to food as fuel. This is similar to the embedding of hospitality as more than just shelter, elevating the notion of hospitality to that of the extraordinary, or even the sacred (see Sheringham and Daruwalla 2007) by creating marketing 'pleasure zones'. As such, everyday lived experience often means that we treat food as fuel, eating as survival or just a means to suppress hunger, experiences marketing illustrates how hospitality, food and dining can be redefined or represented as a hedonistic practice in which we escape the mundane or profanity of everyday lived experience. The myth of food is developed through various themes that are developed below and form the basis of experiences marketing.

■ The Myth of hospitality and food as sacred

The relationship between hospitality, food, the sacred and religion is clearly developed (Hely 2002; Arbury 2005; O'Connor 2005; O'Gorman 2007; Claseen 2007). Experiences marketing utilises a particular marketing language that generates an embedded configuration of hospitality and food within the sacred domain of culture, and becomes part of the 'legitimate art of living' (Reed-Danahay 1996) and can be seen as an example what may be termed a contemporary 'sacralisation ritual' (Belk *et al.* 1989). The experience of hospitality and dining is embedded with ritual and significance (Fantasia 1995; Ferry 2003; Marshall 2005), and the formal dining experience as represented by the formality of the table setting etc., connotes, signifies and directs interpretation by drawing upon the recognised ritualisation and formality of dining (Gvion and Trostler 2008). This ritual of dining creates social order, the ritual acts as a script that is regulated by the order of dishes, the formality of setting and intensity of experience (Marshall 2005). Experiences marketing offers the consumer a 'passage into the sacred' or the 'sacred sphere of excess' (Caillois 1988: 282). The embedded connotations of luxury within experiences marketing, demonstrates a social distinction that enhances social bonds in which dining and hospitality becomes a celebration of society itself (van der Veen 2003) and in the Durkheimian tradition 'sacred'.

■ Tourism and events

Tourism and events as represented within experiences marketing fulfils a social and cultural role and the activity itself becomes a myth (defined by expectation), whereby tourism, events and festivals become 'one of the central means by which the individual makes sense of everyday life' (Lofgren 1999: 6–7). Both the activity and the promise of the activity as represented within experiences marketing offers various escape routes through the creation of a constructed definition or 'configuration' of time and space (Jokinen and McKie 1997; Nelson 2005) that is defined by hedonism, authenticity, fun and escape. This configuration of time and space, between work and play, is a recurrent theme in tourism and events marketing. It highlights the differentiation and significance of the activities and can be seen as a marketing convention to define destinations and experience (see Sturma 1999; Prayag 2009). This signifies a certain binary opposition to everyday lived experience that encourages us to escape, relax or celebrate. Such an approach is clearly witnessed in events marketing which often focuses on the heightening of experience, or carnival, of the spontaneity, exclusivity and extra-ordinaryness of the event. Business events meanwhile. utilise a mixture of both with the profane business element juxtaposed the sacred element of the reward element (food, drink, excursions etc.).

■ The myth of authenticity

Experiences marketing offers tourism and events as a conduit into a more mythical world, where landscape, culture, people and food are more real that the experiences we have in our own everyday life. This approach represents a time and place that is differentiated from everyday lived experience by developing marketing strategies and communications whereby the possibility of escape is signposted for the consumer (Jenkins 2003). As these strategies draw on the embedded significance of tourism and events it creates expected places of tourism, hospitality, events and food marketing. The timeless and spaceless landscapes free the consumer to explore their own emotions through exploring what can be termed 'existential objectivity' and to identify the role of experiences marketing as signifying expected and available time and space in which to explore and seek authentic relations. The significance of events and tourism as an activity become heightened by creating a historical discourse and myth that draws on history, religion, ritual and cultural significance and further embeds its significance within contemporary society.

■ Conclusion

The experience of tourism, events and hospitality is underpinned by a complex historical and cultural discourse that forms the expectations and experiences of the consumer. The location of the practices within a different configuration of time and space, whereby we enter in a liminal world, fuels our imagination to create a myth of experience. This is important as the historical, social, cultural and marketing definition of THEF elevate the experiences beyond the everyday. It justifies the claims that experiences marketing needs to develop and be understood as a specialist field as the definitions and values etc., utilised in other fields such as the marketing of motor cars are not applicable. As marketers we need to understand this definition as it enables us to first, identify the relationship between the product and the consumer and second, it provides us with a set of codes, desires and expectations that should inform both marketing and communication strategies. In conclusion, THEF is a significant activity in which the consumer marks important aspects of their lives. This chapter has argued that as a result of this significance, THEF marketing needs to defined and identified as a specific and specialist area of marketing. The next chapter furthers this claim by examining how traditional marketing practices provide a foundation for the promotion of THEF, but that it arguably lacks the required contextualisation and understanding of the experiences and cultural significance that THEF contains for the contemporary consumer.

Perspectives of Marketing

Introduction

This chapter locates the concept of THEF marketing within current marketing debates. Although this book offers an alternative or complementary approach to contemporary marketing theory and practice, it is important to recognise that much of the literature has been motivated by or has emerged from these debates. Numerous perspectives of marketing exist, and these frame the way in which we think about the nature of marketing and ultimately provide the logic and frameworks that govern practice. This chapter explores these traditional perspectives that have come to dominate contemporary market practice and theory. The chapter also introduces a more culturally orientated critical approach that can strengthen our understanding of experiences marketing.

Marketing the exchange of value

For many years marketing theory and practice has been grounded in what is known as the *exchange paradigm*, or more lately what has been coined *goods dominant logic* (Vargo and Lusch, 2004,2008a). The central idea of exchange is that two or more parties come together (people and institutions engage) in a transaction-orientated relationship to derive some form of sought value from the other entity. This logic is premised upon economic theory that suggests that markets are mobilised and sustained by a scarcity of goods and other resources, and are constituted on the one hand by agents who are able and willing to produce and supply these goods or resources, and on the other, by people or institutions who both need or want them and are able to allocate their own resources to acquire their benefit (Kotler, 1972). So, in a very basic sense, in seeking to satisfy hunger a person will exchange money (the value required by commercial organizations to satisfy shareholder needs) with a food producer for a form of nourishment such as a sandwich. The customer here may also be gaining the benefit of being able to manage the scarcity of time over a busy working day and short lunch break by buying this sandwich from a local supermarket. This is an important element of practice within experiences marketing as products and activities that carry benefits are exchanged with customers for payment and investments of time. (The notion of experience was explored in Chapter 2). This outlines the important value-creating function that THEF organisations perform, but at the same time highlights the fallacy of distributed value that under-lies and provides the catalyst for more recent conceptualisations of marketing which will be defined later in this chapter; namely, the service and interaction perspective.

■ From restricted to complex exchange

The sandwich example described above reflects what Bagozzi (1975) terms *restricted exchange*, which is essentially exchange between two parties. This is the simplest and most basic form of exchange which allows for ease of understanding and does indeed represent some incidences of exchange in sector, such as when an organisation is solely responsible for all of the resources and skills that are combined to produce and take to market a product that is then acquired by a customer for their sole use. However, the nature of exchange is often more nuanced and fragmented. In these cases more than two parties are involved in the exchange process and can be seen to sit in both the demand and supply side spheres of the relationship. These are what Bagozzi (1975) terms *complex patterns of exchange*.

■ Complex exchange and the demand side

In many cases the customer who is directly involved in the transaction will not be the final recipient of the product or service that is exchanged, and therefore the evaluator of its value. This is often the case with the products and activities in the THEF sector. For example, when a purchasing officer representing a company (the customer) identifies, selects, and pays for the accommodation of a travelling executive (the consumer), or when a parent (the customer) purchases an ice cream for an infant (the consumer). In both these cases it will be the consumer (the executive or the infant) who will directly benefit from the value in the product or service that has been purchased from the market on their behalf. However in making this distinction it is worth noting that the customer may also receive some form of indirect benefit from these transactions. In the first example, for instance, the employer of the executive may indirectly benefit from increased productivity and performance due to the rest and recuperation that is enabled by the accommodation whilst the executive is in the field. In the second, the parent may benefit from the respite and momentary freedom from the demands placed on their attention. Thus in these example we can add a third or more parties (i.e., we can add a second or third progeny who could each be the recipient and consumer of their own ice-cream and in the executive accommodation example we could have numerous executives working in the field on behalf of the same organisation who require accommodation and sustenance) to the restricted model of exchange.

These illustrations have also allowed us to neatly differentiate between customers and consumers. While sometimes the customer and consumer is the same person often they are not, however, even though the consumer is the direct beneficiary of the exchanged entity and its value (effects), the customer may also benefit from indirect effects. In the case of the parent and infant for example, if we remove the company who produced and sold the ice-cream from the equation for the moment, we have a classic example of social exchange whereby the confectionery is being offered as amongst other things a symbol of love and affection in exchange for reciprocated affection or good behaviour. If we reinsert the company at this point we can build another picture that further demonstrates the complex nature of exchange. Rather than solely being purchased for the product attributes of flavour and sweetness that provide a combination of hedonic benefits, refreshment and sustenance for the child, the ice-cream is being put into service of behaviour modification by being (re)appropriated as a treat, for incentive or reward. Thus we see the parent receiving direct benefits and value from the purchase of the ice-cream that may be far removed from those intended by the producing company who offered it for exchange. These latter points raise interesting questions about the nature of value (what it is that is actually exchanged), in terms of its character, and how, when and by whom it is produced or created, which are currently central concerns of the marketing academy. Together these have important implications for both marketing theory and practice going forward. Significantly, they bring the notion of exchange as a foundational concept and explanation of marketing into question (for example see Grönroos, 2008, p.309). We will return to these important issues later in the chapter, but for the time being we will continue our focus on the exchange paradigm by examining further instances and forms of complex exchange; this time on the supply side.

■ Complex exchange and the supply side

In the above examples of exchange, we have focused our attention on the producing company and their relationship to customers and consumers. Our attention will now shift to examine examples of complex exchange that exist in the production and supply side sphere. The logic here is that activity would be performed by organisations that have a specialisation for producing and adding further value to a product or service, or alternatively are able to facilitate smoother transactions with customers to better satisfy their needs than would otherwise be possible by the producing company conducting these activities alone. The logic underlying these types of relations are manifold, but in general terms organisations or institutions are inclined to engage in these configurations when they are unable to make provision of a sought value through the utilisation of their own unique skills, resources or knowledge; or alternatively when there is both greater perceived value derived and less cost incurred from actually performing the value creation function independently. Accordingly, amongst other types of arrangements and relationships, we see:

1   Organisations that outsource marketing communications activity to specialist companies such as advertising agencies and production companies, as in the case of the 2012 Warburtons bakers taste test advert which is directed by Smuggler and produced by the agency RKCR/Y&R (creativity-online.com 2012).

2   Those that contract with cleaning companies for related services such as the maintenance and care of hotel rooms or, even facilities management companies to supply air-conditioning and building maintenance activities.

3   Some that may use marketing research companies to provide insight into consumer requirements and the structure and conduct of markets. A good example of this was the relationship between Tesco and Dunnhumby, who until becoming a subsidiary of the retailer itself provided the technology and insight behind the Clubcard.

4   Food manufacturers producing 'own label' products for supermarkets, such as Farmers Boy who produce Morrisons' meat and dairy products

Moreover, an organisation could also contract *in* supporting activities, such as payroll or Human Resource operations that may release the organisation to create further value for its customers by freeing up capacity to concentrate on the things that they are good at doing or specialise in; that is, to focus on their core competence and distinctive capabilities (Prahalad & Hamel, 1990). In most of these cases, a reciprocal relationship will be evident as the contracting company will be receiving the provided and sought benefits in exchange for one or more bundle of value(s) such as payment, an extended or exclusivity contract or arrangement or the exchange of knowledge, information and skills. In this sense, using the lens of the exchange paradigm as a conceptual frame we can see that producing organisations can engage in combinations of downstream supply, upstream distribution, as well as supporting activities (see Porter's value chain, 1980) in seeking to add value and exploit their own distinctive set of skills, resources and competencies through exchange relationships.

Bearing in mind that in this book we are predominantly focusing on consumer marketing and therefore do not wish to get drawn into too much discussion of business to business marketing, the above points are worth indicating and illustrating due to their role in the value creation process for the customer and consumer. For example, travel agents act as intermediaries for the travel companies and as such broker a complex form of exchange with the tourist adding real value to the experience; and no-one can underestimate the importance and role of ad agencies in stimulating consumer behavior and desire for their clients' products and services.

■ Hybrid exchange relationships – the problem of self sufficiency

While it is recognised that the satisfaction of needs are not always conditional upon some form of exchange, such as when a consumer acts to become self sufficient, in contemporary market-based societies most needs are satisfied by and through either total or some form of hybridised exchange (Houston & Gassenheimer 1987). For example, although an individual or family may elect to grow their own food rather than purchase it from a supermarket, or an independently minded traveller may construct an itinerary for a vacation without utilising the services of a travel agent, the market must feature somewhere to facilitate engagement in these practices and in some way be key to their outcomes. So in the case of the former, to grow their own food the individual or family may be reliant on a garden centre for the seeds required to start the process, and then further down the chain become dependent on either the gas or electricity suppliers and producers and retailers of the cooking and dining appliances and utensils that will be required for preparing and consuming the produce as a meal (Houston & Gassenheimer 1987). Equally, the knowledge and skills required for growing food may have origins in market provided resources such as books or a college course and so on (ibid, 1987). This logic will also hold true in the case of the independent traveller who will be reliant on the outfitter market for maps, guidebooks, tents, backpacks and other related resources.

This being the case it is prudent to note that not all exchanges are necessarily and always market transactions. The guidebooks or cookbooks could have been acquired as gifts (e.g. Giesler, 2006; Sherry, 1983) for example. Likewise they could also have been exchanged through swapping (Sherry, 1990), loaned and borrowed or, accessed through donation as part of a ritual of voluntary disposition (Cherrier, 2009). Interestingly, these forms of exchange that, by implication, extend the life of a product are being explored as a means to a more sustainable future. Such practices, it is argued, result in less waste, more efficient use of scare material resources, and mitigate against environmental degradation (e.g. Cooper, 2010).

■ The problem/s for marketing within the exchange perspective

According to Bagozzi (1975) within the exchange perspective marketing has two central and significant problems and these by implication must govern practice. The first is that marketers have to understand the factors that influence and bring about the need or potential for exchange in any given market, that is '…why *and under what conditions* do people and organizations engage in exchange relationships *or not?*'= (38, italics added). Secondly, marketers must be cognizant with how to:

- *create* the conditions to stimulate exchanges

- *resolve* or *satisfy* those needs for exchange that presently exist, or

- dampen or *reverse* existing needs or consumer behaviors.

- Put more simply, marketers must understand how to:

- create valuable propositions to stimulate consumer behaviour;

- deliver value to those who presently require it, or;

- devalue or lessen the appeal of certain goods, activities or market place behaviors, for social, sustainable, or other market benefits.

In accepting Bagozzi's (1975) first problem, and in order to construct a suitable and relevant marketing proposition and offer, marketers must be tasked and focused upon the mechanics and dynamics of their marketplace. They must be aware of the competitive conditions of the market, its infrastructure, and also of the behaviors and requirements of consumers. Equally, marketers also have to understand and appreciate how changes in the macro environment that surrounds their market may influence each of these former elements and which in turn might present possible opportunities for creating value for consumers in ways and areas that may be unexploited or underdeveloped, and that fit within its realm of experience and/or within present or potential capacity of its marketing resources and capabilities.

In recognition of Bagozzi's second problem, marketers must be enabled by a knowledge and capability that allows them to produce/reduce and disseminate/mitigate value. In this instance, we can usefully draw upon the work of Kotler (1972) who has outlined the four basic tasks and functions of marketing to illustrate how value can be created or dissipated, these are: *configuration, valuation, symbolisation* and *facilitation*. We will examine each of these in turn

3

■ Constructing the marketing offer – producing and exchanging value

The marketing offer is the means by which marketers design, give value, symbolize the product within the market, and facilitate the transfer of its ownership or delivery and can be seen to consist of the following process.

■ Configuration

First a marketer is tasked with designing the *social object*, which the term used by Kotler to classify the marketable entity. This can be broadly construed as a physical good/product, service, idea, initiative, destination, place, person or personality. This process and set of activities is called configuration. Here, to be effective the marketer must take account of the features, benefits, activities and performances that will be desirable and most likely to stimulate a preferred response form the intended audience. The social object should also be configured in a manner that is considered to be of superior value than direct or indirect competing offers to mitigate against competitive effects. In some cases however, a marketer may be compelled to make a social object less desirable to an identified target audience. For example the de-marketing of certain destinations where environmental damage is being caused by too many tourists. In these cases the undesirable features and caveats would be the foremost consideration in the configuration process. This practice and process of de-valuing has been coined 'de-marketing' (e.g. Kotler and Levy, 1971) and, as explained below, de-marketing may draw upon the full complement of mix variables as well as much other marketing theory to achieve its goals and purposes (see Kotler and Levy, 1969 for an early but seminal explication of the scope of marketing from the exchange perspective).

It is worth bearing in mind that the concept of configuration captures the theory and nature of a number of allied concepts from the marketing literature. The most obvious of these is the product concept from the 4Ps, but it equally embraces the additional 3Ps of the widened services marketing mix, and the theory underlying the SER-VUCTION model (Eiglier & Langeard, 1975) and that of the Servicescape (Bitner, 1992). So in this respect, this literature and framework posits that perceived and realised value is enhanced through:

1 The configuration of optimal *processes* both frontage (visible) and backstage (invisible) of the service context

2 Planning and managing to get the most from the participants involved in the delivery and performance of the service including the behaviours and interactions of staff and customers/clients

3 The planned and active management of the physical evidence and elements that constitute the servicescape such as ambient conditions, décor and signage (Bitner 1992).

■ Valuation

Secondly, the marketer must construct and apportion a valuation. Logically this must be attractive to the target audience and sufficient to generate the expected demand effects against a range of changeable market or demand conditions. Essentially the expenditure expected from the target audience, be it monetary, temporal, mental or physical effort, and so on, must be considered from their point of view and evaluated vis-a-vis expected value. Equally, marketers ought to consider the range of opportunity costs that may be factored into an evaluation of value, be they economic or otherwise. In respect of maximising the reciprocal value of the social object or experience while allowing for marketing efficiency, the marketer must also be mindful that the optimal (positive or negative) value for the target audience vis-à-vis competitors must be achieved with a sensible cost or minimum cost structure to the marketer's institutional home, to maintain competitive advantage. Likewise the valuation must be favourable against those of directly or indirectly competing social objects or substitutes (this must include the behavioural manifestations related to public health marketing and promotion, and sustainable tourism, etc.).

■ Symbolisation

Experiences marketing utilizes a specific language that draws from a wide range of historically embedded words and images that are used to underpin the marketing and advertising of tourism, events and hospitality. This area is often overlooked and has not been academically developed at the same pace as other areas of marketing; as such, this book has dedicated a chapter to the Semiotics of Experiences (see Chapter 8) and so will not elaborate much here. At this point, we will simply offer the explanation that symbolization refers to the processes and practices of embedding and producing symbolic significance, in terms of meaning/s or informational value that can be transferred, or added to, the social object by the marketer through, amongst other things, design, communication processes and activity, and valuation. The attached meanings can be desirable, repellent, or otherwise dependent upon the marketers' goals and intentions. This process will also incorporate decisions about how, where, when, in what frequency, and by which media to delivery these messages and communications.

■ Facilitation

Fourth and finally, the marketer can add value by making the acquisition or location for the performance and delivery of the social object more convenient and accessible for the target audience, Kotler (1972) terms this as 'facilitation'. Here, issues concerned with range and distance in relation to perceived value and the possible value diminishing prospects of expending effort, time and money ought to be considered. It is worth noting that ease of access is not always positively correlated with value, and as in the case of some social objects, the reverse is often true. Those objects and performances that are perceived as luxury, rare or scarce are examples of this. Often in these cases, the effort, time, money and uncertainty of whether one will ultimately gain access to an activity or performance, or ownership of the desired object adds value in itself, by enhancing the social object's perceived or actual rareness and scarcity. In some cases, a marketer may also be acting to remove a social object from the market or impede access to it. In these instances the employed tactic could be to devalue the social object by somehow making it difficult to access or acquire, or by being selective of who, or when one has access, and the conditions by which they are granted access.

In accordance with this framework the focus and activity of marketers ultimately resides around three core themes and concerns.

- Purchasing or acquisition and the stages and processes leading to this.

- The satisfaction of consumers by delivering the expected value to them through providing an appropriate product or experience, at a time, location, price, and in the case of services within an environment and time-frame that is agreeable.

- In the instance of apparent dissatisfaction recovery of the situation through service guarantee, product recalls or returns policy.

■ Kotler's framework and its relationship to the marketing mix/es

Despite its age, Kotler's (1972) four part exchange framework fruitfully resonates with both the elementary building blocks of marketer created value – the *marketing mix* – and many other forms of contemporary value-creating activity and processes related to transactional exchange. In fact we favour this to the more familiar 4Ps framework as it allows the range of applications such as services marketing, place marketing, social marketing, cause related marketing, and public health marketing, to be reflected than just merely those purely of a commercial and manufactured good based nature. This is essential when this book is directed at students and practitioners that cut across each of these categories of marketing and specific sectors. However to aid understanding, and to familiarise the reader with how this framework relates to the more familiar models such as the 4Ps (McCarthy, 1964), the 4Cs (Lauterborm, 1990), or the 7Ps of Booms and Bitner's (1981) services marketing mix, we have included a table that maps the respective concepts in relation to their operational and conceptual similarity (Figure 3.1).

	Lauterborn 1990	Borden 1964 McCarthy 1964	Booms & Bitner 1981
Configuration	Customer/Client Needs	Product	Product Process Physical Evidence Participants
Valuation	Costs	Price	Price
Symbolisation	Communication	Promotion	Promotion
Facilitation	Convenience	Place	Place

Figure 3.1: Frameworks of Marketing Practice

■ Summary: the production and supply of value

To draw the discussion of exchange to a close, it is evident that within this perspective the fundamental business and role of marketing is to influence and attain desired thoughts, feelings, and behaviours in a social unit – be they individuals or organisations – through the creation, communication and delivery of some form of value that is or has the potential to be attractive to them. This is done in order to produce some form of reciprocated value for the institutional arrangement within which the marketer resides and works. In the case of commercial organisations this is normally money or financial return, but may include things like advocacy, or in the case of cause related organisations or initiatives, the return could be a positive behavior change such has choosing healthier food over those that are not, or with destination marketers, the return could be more environmentally or socio-culturally sensitive tourist behaviours. In producing these desired outcomes, marketers must by implication understand the implied and intended market, in terms of its current or potential requirements, what it may or may not value, and its scale, scope, accessibility and durability. To put it more succinctly:

> Marketing is the social process by which individuals and groups obtain what they need and want through creating and exchanging products and value with others (Kotler 2008).

or

> Marketing is the management process responsible for identifying, anticipating and satisfying audience requirements profitably (CIM, 2011)

Please note that we have taken the liberty of used 'audiences' instead of the actual reference to 'customers' to reflect the wider scope of marketing.

We will now move on to examine the next perspective, which is based upon the premise that marketing is an interactive process that is maintained though the exchange of service rather than value.

■ Marketing as interaction and service

This section introduces a perspective for marketing that is profoundly different from that described above, yet is critical to both the process of marketing and our understanding of the role of the consumer. Essentially this perspective moves marketing on from a discipline underscored by exchange of value towards one that can be better explained by the concepts of interaction and the exchange of service, or as Vargo and Lusch (2004, 2006, 2008a, 2008b) posit, a switch from a *goods dominant logic* to a *service dominant logic*. Broadly construed, this perspective sees a reorientation of the nature and roles of market actors and recasts value creation from being an unequivocal management practice to a co-constitutive process between consumers, organisations and their stakeholders. In particular, this orientation de-centres marketing practitioners from their privileged role as value creators to that of facilitators of a value-creation process. Inseparable from this is the concurrent privileging of the marketing audience – be those consumers, clients or otherwise – who switch from being mere targets of marketer-created value to active players and co-creators of personalised value. Thus the audience is moved from a subordinated position in value creation to an ordinate position.

In this respect, value creation can be explored as either a co-constitutive and negotiated practice between two parties such as consumers and marketers, or a practice undertaken solely by consumers themselves. Accordingly marketing can not be merely theorised from the perspective of value(s) being exchanged through transaction, but rather that value(s) is/are either created and negotiated in and through:

1 The interactions between a marketing organisation and consumer.

2 Solely by a consumer in interaction with a marketer provided resource or proposition.

3 Some combination of the two (e.g. Grönroos, 2008, 2011).

Of course here we are mostly focusing on a dyadic company/ customer relationship, which is justified through the main thrust of this text. However as Vargo and Lusch (2008a) correctly point out, this reorientation of marketing to interaction and exchange of service extends across the range of actors who may enter into some form of marketing relationship such as a network or co-service agreement, and thus spans the value chain. For example, the relationship between a restaurant and their suppliers who provide locally sourced food is both mutually supportive and generates various values, by sharing and co-creating a value chain.

In making this conceptual shift (transition) we will demonstrate that many of the foundational constructs and assumptions underlying the exchange paradigm have been recast and reformulated and will follow by arguing that as a result so should the way in which we think about marketing in terms of its nature and essence. The impact of this is that it challenges and reformulates practice across our sectors which must also align with this re-orientation and shift in logic. Importantly, to aid this shift, the language of marketing needs to be recast to accommodate the essence and underlying characteristics and features of this logic. In this sense we will argue in Chapter 5 that standard marketing concepts such as consumer or audience may need revision so as not to obscure, limit and close down thinking.

■ From goods logic to a logic of service

As examined in Chapter 2, experiences marketing needs to be understood within the context of the experiences offered in tourism, hospitality, events and food. Vargo and Lusch (2008a) have gone some of the way in developing this view by understanding that:

1 Service is the fundamental basis of exchange; marketers supply knowledge, skills and resources to consumers for their use and appropriation.

2 Service is exchanged for service; consumers integrate their own knowledge, skills and resources with those offered by the market to create value and experiences.

3 The customer is always a co-creator of value.

As such, the tourist or customer enter into a dynamic process whereby they may be consuming or purchasing a product or service, but are simultaneously evaluating what is provided, and as a consequence play a significant role in the creation of value by deploying their own resources to create their own meaning and uses from their experiences. This being the case however, our sectors allow for different levels and types of consumer engagement in the value creation/production function. Vargo and Lusch (2008a) and Grönroos (2011) for example, distinguish between co-creation and co-production making the argument that these are different concepts. Specifically they maintain that while co-creation always takes place co-production is optional. We will address this important distinction by dealing with each of these important concepts in turn.

Co-creation can be understood through dealing with each entity of the consumer/company dyad separately. First and foremost, value is created in use, and can only be realised by the consumer during and through the process of consumption. For example, tourists who stay at resorts such as One&Only find different meaning and value through consumption, and their experiences could range from the purely romantic and spiritual, to simply rejuvenating oneself and recharging the batteries, through to more ambitious attempts to escape the mundane reality of everyday life. This is the case because consumers are motivated through seeking to accomplish a range of goals and projects that vary and marketers create a space in which they can co-create value. However, for value to be created there must be some resource or combination of resources to be acted upon by the consumer. These resources include all aspects of the marketing offer and mix such as: promotional materials and communication media; the features, and constituent elements of the product or service scape; the mechanics and mechanisms of and for facilitation, such as purchasing procedures and platforms and those for delivery and access, and price. So returning to the examples outlined above, to facilitate romance a consumer may draw upon the provision of candlelit shoreside dining facilities, to escape their quotidian experience a consumer could make use of the bars and social opportunities, while the spa facilities and beaches may help the consumer in their efforts of rejuvenation. These then are what, in many cases, the marketer offers in the form of a value proposition but it is only through their activation that value is realised. Value is only and always created by the consumer through their interaction with a marketplace resource. In this sense value can never be unequivocally created by the company. Rather, it is realised through consumption. The implication of this for THEF companies is that all they can aim for is to offer attractive value propositions for consumers that may prove meaningful and or facilitate the value creation process in, and through acts and processes of co-creation (Vargo and Lusch, 2004).

Co-production on the other hand involves the customer interacting with an organisation through participation in the design, development, or performance of the value offer itself (Vargo and Lusch 2008a, Grönroos 2011). In some cases the customer is often invited into the production process, by engaging in dialogue with an organisation in the design of a new food product or form of packaging as part of a focus group or member of a consumer tasting panel for example, or is indeed inseparable from the actual production and value creation process in the case of many service encounters such as a restaurant meal, a staged packaged holiday experience such as those offered through the Sunsail brand, or attending a music or food festival. These issues have been widely discussed in the literature on services marketing, and led to Booms and Bitner (1980) extending the 4Ps framework to 7Ps. This was undertaken to reflect the inseparable nature of some service encounters that bring about the interaction between customers and service delivery staff and other customers who are both partaking in, and producing the experience simultaneously. Being part of an audience at an event or having a meal in a restaurant is an illustration of this, as in each of these cases a consumer is integral to the ambience of the experience, thus creating value for the other customers and the business. According to this logic, the process and extent of value co-production that is evident across the experiences offered by the THEF sector can range from extensive and wide ranging to very little or none at all (Vargo and Lusch, 2008a). So for instance, on the one hand, the food shopper engaging with a supermarket may be solely self sufficient in terms of navigating the isles to fill their basket and then engage in checking out the items using the bar code reading self service tills. Thereby, they conduct much of the value producing activity themselves, through interacting with the physical resources and signposting that are part of the store design and layout. Obviously in this example we can see the extensive 'behind the scenes' value facilitating activity that are intrinsic to, and essential to the customer performing their in-store value producing activities. On the other hand however, in cases such as formalised fine dining experiences the consumer will have little room to produce value. That is to say the balance of value is created and delivered by the restaurant. This was especially the case with Chef Ferran Adrià's infamous elBulli restaurant concept, where a customer's only real choice was whether to join the waiting list to get a table or not. If successful in this apparent lottery, consumers got to "enjoy a five-hour meal of thirty-some completely original, whimsical dishes prepared by Adrià and his team of thirty to forty cooks" (Hanna, 2009). In witnessing this multisensory spectacle however, diners were expected to sacrifice their sovereignty and agency of choice to the creative freedom and expression of Adrià and his team.

The implications of the service and interaction perspective for marketing are profound as they challenge the essence and value of particular marketing frameworks and practices. For example, the approach to market segmentation aggregates consumers on their collective responses to various marketing stimuli, such as the value 'contained' in a product (see Holt 1997 for critique of the container metaphor and products) or responses to promotional based offers (e.g. Wind, 1978). As such the limitation in this approach motivates us to rethink the way in which we try to make sense of our audiences and marketing generally. Again we explore these issues in depth later in Chapters 4, 6 and 7).

The value that is generated by both co-creation and co-production is located within the interactive relationship between the marketers, the company and the consumer. There are a number of variables that impact upon this interrelationship, and the most significant of these is the cultural context of the exchange and interaction. In view of this we will now move on to discuss our last perspective for marketing; marketing as a cultural process and practice.

■ Marketing as a cultural process and practice

The notion that marketing can be understood broadly as a cultural process and practice rests upon the assumption that we live in a culturally constituted world (McCracken, 1986; Moisander and Valtonen, 2006; and Penazola, 2000). This refers to the notion that the world we inhabit is constructed from and made intelligible to actors, in our case marketers, consumers and other significant marketing stakeholders, through cultural codes, categories, narratives and discourses. By these, we mean the symbols and systems of meaning and representation that are shared amongst and relevant to members of a particular culture. For example, it is argued that we live situated lives within a network or web of imbricated cultural meanings that frame the way we think, feel, and act in the world, and which also frame and constrain the possibilities of thought, feelings and action in this world (Arnould and Thompson, 2005).

As a result, marketing can be seen as a cultural practice in which marketers engage in a process of, (re) or (de)constructing and (re) circulating systems and units of meaning to consumers or other targets of their activity, such as their shareholders or internal audiences. Put succinctly, marketers are conceived as cultural intermediaries (Moisander and Valtonen 2006). McCracken (1986, 71) demonstrates this by offering 'a theoretical account of the structure and movement of the cultural meaning of consumer goods', whereby, marketers and wider elements of the fashion system are seen as disseminators and distributors of meaning and values. This model posits that meaning moves from the culturally constituted world, through to consumers via the mediating practices of advertisers, marketers, and the wider media, who purposively imbue products with these meanings and value(s) through their practices. Meaning resides 'in the world' in relation to certain places, times, practices, colours, artefacts, music styles, people, personalities, celebrities and so on (McCracken, 1989), which have significance to specific individuals and communities. That is to say, there is a shared pre-understanding across and between different cultures, market segments or interpretive communities in terms of what these entities symbolise. Accordingly these are utilised in adverts and in the design of packaging, etc. to award products and servicescapes with significance and values that are attractive and meaningful to consumers in terms of their potential as useful cultural resources for the accomplishment of specific goals and projects. These goals can include:

- Furnishing, reinforcing and protecting consumers independent and collective identities (e.g. Arsel & Thompson, 2011), for instance that of the foodie, independent traveller, wine connoisseur, skier or snowboarder, and even gender identities (Goulding and Saren, 2009).

- The attainment and construction of specific lifestyles (Holt, 1997), e.g. the health lifestyle (Cockerham, 2005) or the bohemian or hipster lifestyle.

- The accomplishment of specific life projects and themes such as, to follow a morally responsible and ethical life, to act globally whilst thinking locally, or to be a caring mother and successful executive and wealth creator simultaneously (Thompson, 1996).

- Seeking out community ties or links with like-minded others as in the case of coffee aficionados (Kozinets, 2002), lovers of chocolate spreads (Cova, & Pace, 2006), Goths, Trekkers or X-Philes (Goulding and Saren, 2009; Kozinets, 2001;2007;1997), this sector of planned events like the 'Star Trek: Las Vegas Convention' or 'Whitby Gothic Weekend' are often where the community ties and links are most richly experienced and (re)created.

- Helping consumers to reconcile and resolve significant cultural contradictions and paradoxes and threats to their identity and sense of existential security (Holt and Thompson 2004, Holt 2004b) by participating in brand sponsored self-organising events like HOG (Harley Davidson Group) meets, drinking Jack Daniels, (Holt, 2006), or eating Ben & Jerry's Ice-cream (Holt & Cameron, 2010). The significance here being that these activities or brands are fabricated around cultural templates or myths that act as alternatives or salves to dominant ideologies or lived experiences of consumers. For example, Ben & Jerry's draws on a challenger code and expression of back to the land and anti-corporation, that is appealing to US liberal consumers who feel alienated by corporate structures, ideology and relationships. The former examples collectively reflect the outlaw, gunfighter or frontier myth of the US which offer more comfortable templates of masculinity for some male consumers who wish to (re)assert themselves and experience freedom, against the backdrop of forces that are perceived to be emasculating them.

While the world and marketplace is understood culturally, it is not to say that we are imposing a singular cultural deterministic lens to the thoughts and actions of consumers, in the sense that all consumers interpret products and service-scapes in the same way. To be precise, we do not subscribe to an exchange perspective of culture whereby marketers construct the meanings of their products, which are then transferred to, and accepted by consumers at the moment of purchasing. Rather the cultural approach we adopt within this book dovetails with the service logic of marketing in that the meaning of goods and service are co-created and produced by consumers through their interactions and experiences with the marketplace in different and changing settings, situations and contexts, which in turn are refracted by and through different cultural discourses (Arnould, Price, & Malshe, 2005). Thus like Hall (1997), Thompson and Haytko (1997), Arnould and Thompson (2005) before us, we offer a view that marketplace meanings, which include the meanings of adverts, products, servicescapes and so on, are negotiated and mediated between marketers, consumers and their respective stakeholders. This mediation takes place both through their interactions with each other and with their resources, and in interaction with their respective socio-historic and culturally mediated contexts that animate and furnish their interpretive resources and repertoires. In this manner, marketer produced meanings can either be accepted from the marketer's perspective almost verbatim, rejected altogether, or (re)appropriated. Thus, in alignment and broad agreement with Holt (1997, 334) within the cultural perspective of marketing, products (the social object/s), in the broadest sense can be conceived as "polysemic symbolic resources that allow for significant variation in consumer interpretation and use".

◼ Conclusion

This chapter has examined traditional and emerging approaches to marketing. This has allowed us to evaluate and locate the critical approach adopted within the remainder of the text. The work of Kotler, Vargo & Lusch and others, has provided an important foundationstone in contemporary practices. However these approaches are sometimes limited because they do not fully recognise the cultural significance of marketing per se. As identified in the previous chapter, THEF fulfills a significant role in contemporary society, and in order to understand, locate and effectively market such experiences it has to be located within a culturally orientated framework. Consumers do not merely go to markets to satisfy latent needs and wants, nor solely to create value. Often, amongst other things, they are there to engage in a complex consumption process that inform and (re)produces their identity. It must be stressed that in order to develop a holistic approach to marketing, we do not discount the traditional exchange perspective or the more recent service dominant logic, but incorporate and enhance these within the cultural and social context of the market and world more generally. The next chapter explores this further by examining the role of consumer resources within the THEF sectors.

4 Consumer Resources and THEF Experiences

■ Introduction

This chapter explores how individual consumers utilise a set of resources to negotiate and form their experiences with THEF products and activities. The traditional approach to understanding consumers including marketing resources is normally located at the macro level, assumptions are made that all members of a demographic or socio-economic group posses the same or similar resources. However, this chapter makes the assertion that individual consumers all possess different resources of various kinds and deploy them in individual personal ways. The result of this is that it is important that we can locate and place the consumer in a micro framework of resources and practices, as it is only then that we can locate and understand the consumer's capabilities and relations to marketing and products. A number of resources and practices will be examined below. These resources also inform a number of other chapters in this including the location and status of consumers by defining their group position as explored in Chapter 6.

■ An outline of the Theory of Resources

The service logic of marketing is predicated on the notion that value is created through the integration interaction of marketing resources (products, activities, deeds, and communications etc.)

with those of the consumers. This interaction based perspective mirrors the theories of the cultural perspective that maintains that marketers produce cultural resources that consumers incorporate into their lives through the deployment of their own resources and consumption practices. Integral to both these perspectives are what Vargo and Lusch (2004) call operand and operant resources.

- Operand resources are those that a consumer acts upon to create value and would include a marketplace object or activity itself and their money, time, allocative spaces or material resources (Arnould *et al.* 2006).

- Operant resources on the other hand are those that a consumer deploys to act upon operand resources to create value (Vargo and Lusch 2004).

In this chapter these specifically include a consumers stock of knowledge and skill (Arnould *et al.* 2006). In most cases a combination of operand and operant resources are integrated alongside those offered through the marketplace to create meanings and value. For example a consumer, staging a dinner party will draw upon their ability to cook (resources of knowledge and skill) and utilise their kitchen appliances, cookbooks and utensils (material resources), to produce a meal for their friends (social resources) using items they purchased from the supermarket (marketplace resources) using their money or vouchers (financial resources).

Having outlined the role and significance of consumer resources we now turn to describing the nature of each of these and their relevance in producing THEF experiences. We will begin by looking at consumer operand resources, which include financial resources, time, material resources and space. This will be followed by an examination of consumer knowledge and skills that constitute the consumer's operant resources.

■ Financial resources

The financial resources a consumer possesses has a direct impact upon their behaviour, as the type of experiences you engage in are dependent upon how much money you have to spend on THEF. Consumption is both enabled and constrained simply through access to economic resource or capital. Whether these resources are earned through the sale of one's labour or otherwise it is a simple equation; a consumer either has discretionary or disposable financial resources to allocate to THEF experiences or not. Put simply, discretionary monies are those that remain after a consumer has met their financial obligations. These would normally include mortgage or rent payments, the basic provision of food and household utility goods, household bills and other personally chosen obligations such as pensions, savings and so forth. Importantly, it is discretionary spend that is of most interest to marketers of THEF experiences and products because for most people they sit outside the realm of normal everyday experience, are non-essential and in some cases even considered as luxuries.

Writing this subsequent to the credit crunch, and in the midst of the continual global financial crisis, we must also give consideration to the consumption possibilities that are enabled through access to credit. Coupled with the economic boom between 1994 and 2004 and the relaxation of credit constrains, the world has witnessed a consumer credit explosion that is evidenced by the huge number of credit cards and loans that were available during this period (Brown, Taylor and Price, 2005).

In February 2012, net UK personal debt including mortgages stood at a staggering £1.47 trillion (creditaction.org), and a recent report by Aviva, based on a randomised study of 10,000 people aged between 18 and 55, places unsecured household debt at £7,944 (Papworth 2012). Furthermore, it seems we cannot underestimate the role of credit in the lives of contemporary consumers as a recent study argues that the practice of having credit and accumulating debt has become normalised in contemporary consumer society (Peñaloza and Barhart 2011). In accordance with this, research by Bernthal *et al.* (2005) identify that credit cards have become a primary resource for facilitating consumption-orientated lifestyles that are qualitatively different from those that would be achievable without them; they enable a higher level of participation, a consumer can do more and elevate their consumption to previously unachievable experiences. Often THEF products and experiences are classified as a luxury and were paid for through some form of credit. Accordingly, while we do not necessarily advocate it, a consumer can take more frequent and better holidays, eat out more or enjoy a greater range of added value foods than previously permissible, with the only constraint being the potential stored within their credit resources.

Nonetheless access to credit and unmitigated use may induce the burden of debt and as a resultant remove a consumer from the market. This may be through either, or a combination of:

(1) Reductions in discretionary spend through prioritising the service of loans and other forms of debt.

(2) Heightened levels of perceived financial risk, and felt ontological insecurity of the financial future.

(3) The inability to shuffle debt among financial instruments.

(Bernthal *et al.* 2005)

Perceived risk, and arguably others on the above list, are seemingly being experienced by many consumers, as fears and uncertainty fuelled by the economic outlook has resulted in a decline in customer confidence. Thus, against this backdrop we are simultaneously witnessing the growth of food discounters such as Aldi, Lidl and Netto (Wood 2011), growth in volume sales of crisps and small treats but significant drops in sales across the hospitality, travel and leisure sector.

■ The resource of time

Just as you need a surplus of cash to engage in THEF activities you also need a surplus of time. Time is becoming a increasingly critical and scarce consumer resource. This is certainly the case for the THEF sectors in terms of the design of their marketing offer which can be broadly classified as high involvement services, products or experiences that are extremely time consuming. To go on holiday, attend a concert, take a romantic restaurant meal, or stay at home to cook a meal from scratch all require significant investments and allocations of time. This is not only the case for the actual activity itself but also the planning and preparation that is required for each of these things. Not only this, consumers are also often caught up in the process of waiting to engage or experience THEF activities and products. We wait in-line to get on to rides in theme-parks such as Disneyland or Alton Towers, we queue at the tills in supermarkets, and countdown the time before we can escape on holiday. Obviously there is huge variation in the time that would be committed to the broad range of activities or experiences that constitute our sectors and many time-saving devices that may balance the demands placed on consumers.

Consumers all possess different time equity, the job they undertake, the pets they own, the age of the children they have, all impact upon how much surplus time they have to engage in THEF experiences. Our increased access to technology has not freed up time rather it has blurred the boundaries between work and free time or home, the ability to check your e-mails on your phone or access work materials via the internet have constructed a new set of elements that impact upon our time resource. In many respects the market often steps in to provide consumers with time-saving devices and convenience products to manage the lack of time possessed by consumers. The introduction of apps by airlines to streamline the booking in process or self-service checkouts in shops all alleviate the time constraints surrounding THEF experiences.

As a reaction to this there has been the development of a movement that uses slowness as its core theme, there is evidence that some consumers seek out the opposite and opt for a slow life or leisurely experiences that allow them to resist the pressures of the modern world. This is reflected in trends such as the slow food movement. In this sense it can be seen as a move to resist the 'consumption ethic'. This type of behaviour is often facilitated through down-shifting or engaging in practices of voluntary simplicity (Bekin *et al.* 2005). This type of consumer experience is often overlooked in the marketing literature which tends to mostly focus on experiences that can be classified as 'extraordinary' (Carù and Cova 2003).

■ Space as resource

The most obvious application of space as a consumer resource in value creation is related to food. Kitchen cupboards, freezers, refrigerators, and counter top area all enable the food consumer in a very practical and obvious way. The former three examples, for instance, grant the consumer the capacity to store a wide range of food items under varying conditions, minimising the need to con-duct frequent shopping trips and fragmented purchases. Ample storage space also facilitates bulk purchasing and the ubiquitous weekly or 'big' shop. Having access to a vehicle with large volumes of storage capacity performs a similar value creation function for the consumer, as does a wine cellar for a wine collector or con-noisseur. Equally, counter-top space and work area are invaluable for those who have a preference for scratch cooking or preserving produce through pickling, jam making etc.

Dining practices and the range of related normative consumer goals are similarly structured by allocations of space. Extending an invitation to friends or professional colleagues for dinner, the opportunity to host a children birthday party, or feast at Christmas, or being able to sit up to a dining table for breakfast with the family prior to leaving for work are enabled or constrained by this resource. On top of other things, opportunities to meaningfully interact with the family to share experiences, build family identity and values, celebrate, play or build networks in pursuit of career goals or aspirations, are therefore all facilitated and mediated by and through this type of allocative space and its integration with food commodities and related food practices, performances and rituals.

Moving outside the house, owned or rented space such as a garden or allotment, or having membership and access to a community agricultural project and accompanying resources offer further spatial resource for value creation. For example they can be utilised for growing your own food and composting. These resources and practices for example may be used by a hard pressed and financially constrained consumer to make meaningful and valuable savings to their food budget and expenditure. They could also be deployed in service of constructing a foodie lifestyle or maybe they are being accumulated as part of a plan and life project to down-shift to a simpler, self-sufficient and slower pace life (Bekin *et al.* 2005).

However we can find examples of physical space relevant to travel and events. The most obvious of these for the traveller or tourist, or indeed a festival goer, is related to luggage. Luggage delimits what can and cannot be taken on a trip, in many cases this may have a direct correlation with personal material resources such as the size and quantity of suitcases, holdalls, backpack or car boot/trunk, but in many cases it could be structured by the chosen mode and means of travel. Constrained resource exist in terms of baggage and how much one can take and store on a plane without incurring a financial penalty or have to pay a surcharge. In this sense space is important in the means end chain of value creation. In other cases it could be related to accommodation space.

The potential of consumption and how and what value can be created or experienced will often relate to the scale and scope of accommodation space. In some cases a consumer may have the benefit and luxury of a suite and in others they may be cramped into a small double room that barely has the space to store luggage. Similarly a consumer may be taking a holiday in a large static caravan, gîte or chalet or confined to a tent, shared youth hostel bedroom or small mobile caravan. In terms of the latter however, dependent upon weather and where the tent is pitched or caravan parked, it could be argued that the consumer is unconstrained by space in terms of the potential of the great outdoors. Obviously with each of these examples there is a significant relationship to material and financial resources. Under normal conditions, the market price of suites and gîtes is greater than those for small hotel rooms or hostel accommodation of similar aesthetic and material standard, likewise the spatial resources and potential of a tent or caravan are determined by those presently owned, borrowed or rented.

■ Supporting material resources

It is quite possible to create an endless list in relation to this concept. It is fair to say that with each of the sectors covered here, an experience is mobilised and only made possible through the integration of a relevant and related selection of a consumer's material resources. These could be those that are presently owned in the stock of consumer possessions or those that need to be acquired through purchase or otherwise, to enable or support the consumption experience. That is they are often if not always a necessary condition for value creation. What is more they also perform a role in structuring the possibility and scope of value creation and meaning production. In studies of tourism for example, cameras extend the boundaries of a consumer experience allowing for it to be shared and (re)created infinitely over the future and a consumers life-course (Crouch and Desforges 2003). Walking boots liberate consumers and allow for the mastery of space and challenging environments (ibid.). Cookbooks structure identity and legitimise gendered behaviour (Brownlie and Hewer 2007). Clothing and other material resources allow consumers to engage in identity performance and seek acceptance and legitimacy, in particular, consumer cultures and context such as raving or snowboarding. Meanwhile maps, GPS and mobile technology allow consumers to manage significant risk and uncertainty and engage in activities that previously would have proven exclusionary.

■ Social resources

Like the other resources covered in this chapter, those that are social take numerous forms and are deployed and acted upon by consumers in many ways. We identify three broad types here. These are:

1 People and networks from which consumers seek referral, knowledge or information about a product or service, such as in the form of word of mouth (WOM).

2 Those that are either integral as participants to the episode of consumption itself or those involved in delivery.

3 Those that are needed as reference points for the personal or collective realisation of value and meanings.

There exists a number of social resources that aid selection and sharing of experiences and value propositions, many of these are of particular importance to the THEF sector as they communicate experience from one consumer to another.

■ Word of mouth

An invaluable resource when considering the evidence, is that WOM is the most persuasive and influential form of marketing communication (Kozinets *et al.* 2010). As it is often impartial, actively sought, and in many cases located within a social network or sphere were the consumer has strong ties, familiarity and a high degree of shared personal and social characteristics and commit-ment, WOM is perceived to be relatively more trustworthy, reliable and credible (Brown *et al.* 2007). This is especially the case when consumers defer to family, friends, work colleagues or other close acquaintances. Equally, word of mouth mostly takes the form of an active dialogue so the consumer can extract or share informa-tion that is mostly relevant to them in terms of their motives, and preferences relative to a product, activity or experience. However, it appears that new forms of WOM are emerging that challenge the traditional view and model of close ties and familiarity, immediacy being the overriding criteria through which one can understand the dynamics of this form of communication.

■ Social media

The growth of social media which is mobilised by Web 2.0 social platforms and tools, combined with the rapid development and diffusion of mobile technology is undoubtedly transforming the ways in which we communicate generally, and, more specifically, with whom we seek out marketing information and share our own consumption experiences and outcomes. This is clearly evident in all of our sectors where consumers have access to:

- specific consumer social media platforms such as Tripadvisor®, foursquare or Moneysupermarket;
- generic social tools like Facebook, Google+ and Twitter
- sector focused social apps like Foodspotting and the artofbackpacking;
- blogs dedicated to specific THEF products and experiences such as the Glastonbury Festival (http://www.glaston-buryfestivals.co.uk) or specific consumption practices, for instance, alt.coffee.

These are providing the platform for enhanced and augmented consumption experiences, while simultaneously offering ample marketing opportunities and challenges. Kozinets (1999, 2010) for example has modelled the numerous ways in which people interact with online consumption communities and the motives that underlay and direct their interactions and behaviour. The position a consumer adopts within these communities will define the level of social resource they possess. Kozinets went on to identify the various social positions consumer may adopt, these include:

Tourists

Tourists are those someone who have infrequent contact with the community, a low commitment to it and very weak ties. They merely drop in occasionally or visit for information when it is needed for instrumental reasons, such as the lead up to a purchase. The community therefore acts as an informational resource that may be included in a search or assessment of a specific product, brand, activity or service, or of others' experiences of them. These would be evaluated alongside a range of other sources that may be included in a Tourist's information search such as an organisation's advertisements or web-pages and more traditional forms of word of mouth. The communication in these instances and episodes is extremely didactic and unidirectional. In many cases the Tourist would merely search through and engage existing information contained in extant posts, with other interaction limited to posting specific and direct questions related to the functional attributes of a product or a consumer's experiences with it/them.

Minglers

Minglers are more active in the social aspects and life of the community. They become participants. Although drawn in, in similar ways to the Tourist, in the search for product knowledge and information, the motive branches out to be inclusive of congenial interaction, interpersonal experience and value. The Mingler will thus use the community as a resource to build virtual friendships, social capital, and relationships. Importantly, in this case, the social experience will be considered to be equally if not more valuable than the information role and resource that the community provides. In actual fact, in most cases, the social experience will transcend the very reason as to why the Mingler was drawn to the community in the first place. This was ultimately to find out about and discuss the product or because they had initially shown interest in it. Accordingly the link becomes more important than the thing; the product or consumption experience (Cova, 1997). Under these conditions the social resource itself ultimately ends up providing the majority if not all of the value and meaning for the consumer.

Devotees

We next have devotees, whose interest and interaction with the community is fully consumption orientated and product related. They will be engaged mostly with the endorsement and critique of products and services and occupied in protracted discussions related to consumption experiences. In view of this, the Devotee will typically hold the most influence over the tourist by providing the majority share of product-related information and reviews within the community. This will be compounded by their authoritative self-positioning as 'expert' consumers which will be evident through the style of their dialogue and interactions. They will also be the most appealing and valuable to the tourist by the fact that less consumption orientated work will be required in accessing desired information. A Devotee's posts will be focused specifically on consumption, efficiencies can be made and time saved by not having to sift through social chit-chat that will litter the posts of Minglers and Insiders.

Insiders

These are extremely active in both realms of experience in the community. They engage in product and consumption related dialogue in a manner on par with a Devotee and, like the Mingler, are active in the social aspects of the community. In this respect, Insiders have multiple motives attached to their engagement with the community. Value and meaning is derived in equal measure from the relational, recreational and informational modes of experience and interaction. As a result, the Insider is an important and critical social resource for all of the other participants and interlocutors engaged in online consumption orientated activity and engagement, making them, along with Devotees, an important target for marketing activity. What is more, given their manifold roles, that encompass friendship, play, community maintenance, and information disseminator, they may better fit the typical and traditional model of a credible WOM source. In the sense that they will be perceived to have expertise, be less prone to bias and consequently, be considered more trustworthy (Brown *et al.* 2007).

■ Social resources integral to episodes and experiences of consumption

■ Value creation and meaning production

We now focus on those social resources that are inclusive to the value creation process itself. Here we include those that are either co-participants in the consumption process itself or those that are central to the staging or performance of the experience. With some obvious exceptions, much of what constitutes the experience that is offered by the THEF sector can be classified as social activities, performances and experiences. This is the case whether it is an excursion to Glyndebourne for the annual opera festival, a week away with friends on a package holiday, a family outing to Nando's restaurant or a trip to the supermarket with the children for the weekly shop. Amongst other things, these then are collective experiences that may be pursued as an expression of fandom or devotion, the pursuit of hedonistic play, or merely as utilitarian ritualised practice for feeding the family. In this sense, value and meaning is created within and through a social unit, and is critically dependent upon the actions and interactions of those inclusive to it.

The social unit and those that are either presently or potentially integral to it are therefore the consumer resource. While there are exceptions to this rule and logic, these are limited in scope. However once out of the home environment you enter a social context that brings you into contact with others. Entering the supermarket, the foyer of a hotel, or walking the Great Wall of China are inherently socially mediated experiences. Even shopping online becomes a social encounter at some stage when your food is delivered to your door or if you have to make an enquiry or lodge a complaint with the retailer over the telephone. What is clear is the interaction that takes place between the stakeholders in THEF experiences, for example, host and guest, air steward and passenger, the constitutes a resource.

■ Service delivery personnel as social resource

Through an examination of the actions and behaviour of employees and service personnel, Winstead (2000) offers insight into how they could be considered as social resources for value creation and customer satisfaction. He outlines three categories of behaviour that are seemingly manifest and displayed by valued service personnel that could be activated by consumers, these are, concern, civility and congeniality. In this sense, consumers could activate these behaviours and role performances in the following ways:

- Seek information, clarification or reassurance about a specific element or episode of their experience. So for example a consumer could consult with a sommelier or wine steward to explore and make recommendations of what wine would best complement their choice of food, or a grocery shopper could simply ask a sales floor clerk or assistant where they could locate a specific food item. Likewise a family taking a family holiday could consult a service desk clerk of their hotel for ideas and recommendations of what to visit and explore on a particular day of the week. Or alternatively they might seek an upgrade due to some felt dissatisfaction with their present accommodation.

- To feel valued and receive a level of service that is deemed appropriate and relevant to their expectations vis-à-vis their relative investment in that activity. This would also include the propensity for staff to manage the wider service environment and context to similar ends. So while in this case a service delivery agent may not be being directly activated by a consumer, they are still a critical resource for them in experiential terms.

- Engage in social intercourse to pass time or strike up a convivial conversation. In this respect being able to engage in idle chit-chat with a member of bar staff could be significant to enhancing the experience of a travelling executive. Of course, this form of customised service should not be to the detriment of others who may resultantly feel ignored.

Drawing on the work of Arnould *et al.* (1998) we can extend this framework and add a fourth category, which is communicative staging. While this can include all communications media that constitute a servicescape or environment, such as the large menu boards in McDonald's restaurants or signs that direct consumers to washrooms, those communications that are highly dependent on the behaviour of staff would necessarily include a great deal of interpersonal interaction. In terms of these latter, communicative staging can range from a highly scripted and commercially punctuated performance, through to flexible and authentic dialogue. In their study of the wilderness servicescape and white water rafting excursions for example, Arnould *et al.* (1998) demonstrate how a natural environment is commercially appropriated for the enjoyment and consumption of adventure seekers through the scripts and role performances of the raft guides. Not only do service delivery personnel bring the experience and the environment to life for participants through narrative framing and storytelling, they also act to make it safe and magical (Arnould and Price 1993). In a similar way the reps of Thomas Cook's Club 18–30 are instrumental to the communicative staging of hedonistic experiences and extreme play in holiday resorts and destinations across Europe. They are simultaneously tasked with organising and leading activities, mediating between hotel suppliers and the customer, and solving consumer problems and issues. What is more, right from the moment of the first encounter with consumers through to the last they are required to embody and perform the espoused values of the 18–30 concept itself.

■ Customers as resources for consumers

Next we consider the role of customers as resources for consumers. In a similar manner to service personnel, with the majority of THEF products and activities, customers are integral to their staging and production. Ultimately customers play a decisive role in creating the experience for others. Bitner *et al.* (1997: 195), for instance outline a variety of roles that consumers play in this process, these being:

- The customer as productive resource, for example where customers create an atmosphere in an empty restaurant.

- The customer as intrinsic to quality, satisfaction and value, this is seen when a customer needs to perform a specific role him or herself for the services to take effect and be evaluated positively. Ordering from a menu, negotiating the supermarket to fill the shopping basket or using a self-service till is reflective of this.

- The customer as competitor to service organization, for example where a customer publically complains about the service or meal, thus causing a scene and de-valuing the product and experience for others.

They go on to argue that these roles are not mutually exclusive and that a consumer can be performing one, two or all of these in and across different consumption situations and contexts. Thus *other* consumers become a resource through which valuable and meaningful experiences are created, heightened and realised or conversely through which they are impeded, vitiated or destroyed. This poses an interesting relationship for an organisation where the customer becomes a resource for the firm, where their behaviour needs to be managed for the benefit and experience of others (Gronroos 2011). It is not surprising therefore that Grove and Fisk made the wry observation that:

> Consumers learn through experience that some service organizations expect their audience to arrive bathed, shaved, coiffed and dressed in formal style. Such expectations are common for gourmet restaurants... *or...* the opera.
>
> (1992: 6, emphasis added)

■ Other orientated consumption: I shall be your mirror

The next social resource under review relates to what is termed other orientated consumption (Holbrook 1999). In essence this is consumption that requires other people to be integral to a consumers frame of reference for value to be experienced and realised. These are necessary others that are required to legitimise and qualify a consumers status play, identity performance or lifestyle. This theme has been fully developed in Chapter 6 (which examines how consumption expresses identity and membership to groups or consumption tribes so the subject will not be fully developed in this chapter). Equally status play requires relevant others to prove meaningful, in status orientated or conspicuous consumption, goods and services are purposively selected and consumed that situate and position a consumer within a stratified social order (Veblen [1899] 2007; Holbrook 1999). To take effect, the goods, services and consumption practices must have a social meaning that is ordered and differentiated and collectively understood and shared by others. So with status play or conspicuous consumption, a consensus must exist amongst a social collective of how a specific hotel brand, event, or restaurant concept is different to others in relation to price, luxury, service levels and customisation. Plainly the conspicuous consumer would choose the most expensive, luxurious and attentive in its service offer. This socially mediated consumer behaviour underscores most identity performances and lifestyle consumption practices. For this to take effect and be meaningful, a consumer must be able to make a comparison between themselves and in relation to others, in terms of their consumption choices, tastes, behaviour and practices.

■ Knowledge and skill as consumer resource

Knowledge and skill grant the consumer agency and opportunity within both specialised and generic consumption fields and marketplaces. Likewise, as in the case of the others, deficiency in these resources has the opposite effect creating experiential redundancy across a range of dimensions and contexts. These ideas seem straightforward and obvious when the range of experiences, products, and activities of the THEF sector are taken into consideration. To be an independent traveller or to engage in scratch cooking, necessitates the application and utilisation of particular knowledge and skill sets. To survive the harsh condition of the Black Rock Desert whilst maintaining the ability to (co)create the Burning Man festival through radical self-expression or performance art requires a different set of specialisations (Kozinets 2002b).

The modern marketplace also demands a particular kind of knowledge and set of skills to be a competent and successful consumer. The ability to utilise computers and mobile devices to search out information, download and use apps, or make online bookings and reservations or purchase tickets for an event are but a few examples of this. The ability to juggle financial instruments to make the most efficient use of the marketplace and the products on offer is also useful (Bernthal *et al.* 2005). While on the surface these seem trivial, being basic to the tacit knowledge of most contemporary consumers, we must remember that such understanding and ability is not uniformly shared across all market segments. The third age and the hard pressed particularly struggle to keep pace with these changes in the structure and performance of the marketplace, and may be deficient in the necessary competencies.

Accordingly in our technically mediated world, just keeping up with the rapid changes and innovation of the THEF marketplace requires a particular kind of mastery. Knowledge and skill thus frames agency and mobilises the notion of the sovereign consumer.

While in this section so far, we have mainly focused on those THEF products and experiences that require the application of specialised knowledge and skill, others can be consumed in both a generic or specialised way dependent upon how consumers approach an object or experience and the type of value or meaning they aim to extract from it. Here we can locate products and activities such as wine or beer, exhibitions, festivals and galleries or restaurant meals; for example, studies have examined amongst other things Goth festivals, Star Trek conventions, football matches and baseball games. Within these contexts, the application of specialised knowledge integrated with specific consumer practices and goals clearly distinguish the experience of some from those of others. The Whitby Goth festival for instance provides clear evidence of this (Goulding and Saren 2009). This bi-annual week-long event that takes place in the seaside town where Bram Stoker wrote Dracula is both tourist spectacle and a liminal space or TAZ (temporary autonomous zone) in which engaged participants are able to perform and momentarily experience forms of gender that differ from those experienced in everyday life. By drawing on a range of resources Whitby Goths are able to 'put the curves back into the feminine', blur the boundaries of gender or transgress the normative codes and templates that frame and construct quotidian experiences of sexuality (ibid.: 27). Thus, the integration of knowledge of the festival, codes of dress and the vampire myth, with material and social resources, allows participants to engage in meaningful and expressive identity performances. These motives and experiences clearly differ from those of say a day visitor who may be drawn to the spectacle to gaze or to be entertained by the performances and communicative staging of the engaged participant.

■ Conclusion

This chapter has examined the role of consumer resources and practices in value creation. There is no doubt that these are essential for consumers to engage in the experiences offered by the THEF sectors, but it is also clear that they are necessary for the realisation of individual and collective goals and projects. While the normal tools, concepts and frameworks presently available to marketers for understanding their consumers are significant and valuable, namely those of market segmentation, they do not fully get to grips with how value and marketplace meanings are (re)produced by consumers. Following Holt (1998) we agree that market segmentation often abstracts away the nuance and detail that is central to truly understanding marketplace behaviours and activity, therefore this resource and practice-based perspective offers a resolution. By really getting to grips with the resources and capabilities that mobilise and delimit consumer behaviours across a range of contexts and settings, and by understanding the consumer, the THEF marketer will be well placed to develop and produce marketing strategies that have significance to their consumers' lives and lifeworld. For example in recognising the demands placed on consumers' financial resources, food retailers were quickly able to offer solutions to this problem. What is more, some were able to do this while protecting their consumers identity projects and life themes. Sainsbury's for instance, in recognising the significance of food and its role as a *resource* in constituting and producing family roles and identity produced an advert that promoted its Brands Match range against the backdrop of a narrative of kinship, family solidarity, the patriarchal protective bond between a father and his son, and the love of food. This stands in stark contrast to the normal bland or nondescript messages and meanings associated with budget food products and their associated promotions.

In addition to the commercial applications and potential of the resource-based view of the consumer it may have an equally significant role to play in consumer protection and sustainable market practice. For example policy makers with a stakeholder interest in the THEF sectors may be equipped to produce solutions or intermediate in the market where significant resource deficiencies may either immobilise consumers, limit their potential or place them in harm's way (Arnould *et al.* 2006). Examples of this may include amongst others:

1 Deficiencies in consumer knowledge of the benefits of sunscreens and creams in protecting against skin cancer;

2 Awareness of the nutritional and ingredient constituents of food items on restaurant menus; and

3 Knowledge of the consequences of poor hygiene or sexual practices at festivals.

Chapter 6, develops some of these ideas by examining notions of knowledge and how these forms of THEF knowledge define both the individual consumer and their position within society or culture.

Consumption and the Consumer

■ Introduction

This chapter examines the notions of consumption and consumers, it is important that we understand what is meant by consumption and how we locate the consumer within the consumption process. THEF marketing utilises a complex set of codes, images and strategies to communicate a very particular product or experience, however the consumption of tourism, hospitality, events and even food differs from other products, by the fact that we are dealing with experiences rather than tangible goods such as a car. This chapter helps to locate what is consumed and how this happens. Additionally this chapter locates the consumer by examining their motivations, classification and search for experience that forms a culturally orientated definition of consumption and the consumer.

■ The process of consumption

It is generally agreed the consumption is a process that includes the actions and activities of selection, acquisition, consumption and the dispossession of products, services or experiences (Solomon 2006). It can be asserted that experiences marketing provides a platform for consumers to enter a dream world, in which they can escape the pressures of everyday lived experience, and as such we need to ask the question of when does the consumption process actually begin or is initiated: is it at the point of arriving at a destination? Taking the first mouthful of a meal? When the first band begins to play? Or is it when we read the brochure or examine the website? It can be argued that the consumption process in experiences marketing starts at the initial research stage. Likewise we also need to question when it ends, or indeed if there is a boundary that marks out an end or closure. However, what we can agree on is that the consumer starts with a need or desire to experience something. Under most conditions it is also agreed that consumers seek to satisfy their needs and wants through consumption. As a result, consumption is often theorised as goal orientated behaviour. These four activities as identified in Figure 5.1 warrant exposition to allow marketers to have a better understanding of the way consumer acts within the market.

■ Selection

Selection refers to the means by which consumers seek out information and knowledge about the range of hospitality, tourism and events goods, services and experiences that exist in the market. Historically the information available to the consumer was greatly influenced by marketers and was generated by the organisation through marketing communication channels such as advertisements, brochures etc. Under these conditions the consumer would typically appraise competing offers in the market based upon the claims made by organisations and through other visible aspects of the marketing mix such as for example, prices, discounts and other means of incentivisation or promotion. However as information channels have fragmented over time and new media channels such as Twitter, Tripadvisor and Facebook have emerged, consumers now have many other sources and means to seek out information and to inform their choices. Indeed, whilst consumers have always communicated between themselves through traditional forms of word of mouth, debates and research are currently focusing on the changing shifts of power within market-orientated relationships due to the enabling technologies of social media and the potentials of the World Wide Web, and as such numerous commentators are pointing to a new era of consumer power. These are significant to warrant further discussion and will feature more heavily later in this chapter and at other points in the book. In this sense, there is a numerous consumer-orientated activities that need to be considered.

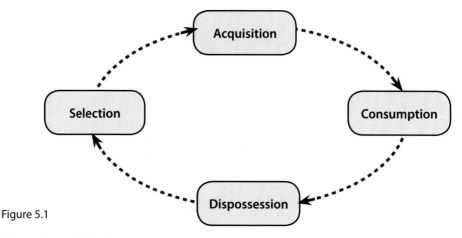

Figure 5.1

■ Acquisition

Acquisition is the next aspect of the consumption process and generally refers to the means by which people acquire or come to possess, either the product, service or experience or the promise of a future consumption experience. Ultimately, this involves some form of marketing exchange. That is the consumer exchanges a unit of vale such as money or a voucher for the benefit of acquiring or consuming something. It is worth pointing out at this stage that the purchaser may not always be the person who ultimately consumes the purchased product. So for example, it may be a gift such as a box of chocolates that may have been purchased or could be a weekend break that has been purchased by an organisation to reward or incentivise a member of staff. In this respect, the purchaser would be the customer of the product and not the consumer. Self-provisioning, gifting, rewards and incentives, prizes and competitions, stand as just a few examples of other ways of acquiring products than purchasing alone.

■ Consumption

The definition of consumption has become nuanced in recent times. Traditionally, and in most works of marketing and organisation theory it is conceived as the process and act of extracting the value from the product, service or experience by the consumer. In a seminal paper, Theodore Levitt (2004) for example espoused the notion that people purchase and consume benefits as he stated: 'People do not buy quarter inch drills they buy quarter inch holes'. The value in these cases is created through the practices and behaviours of organisations in bringing and offering their products to the market. From this explanation, value is created in numerous ways. For example, it could be through the design of the product itself. In other cases, it could be how an organisation has sought to differentiate the product from others that exist in the same market. In this case, under normal conditions the organisation has sought out noticeable needs in the market or has found ways of satisfying needs in superior ways than the competition through processes of innovation or new product development. Alternatively, it could be the way that an organisation chooses to bring the product to the market. Value may be induced by streamlining the means by which a consumer acquires a product. Ticketmaster and other ticket agencies provide added value for organisations who seek to make the act of purchasing tickets more convenient for the customer. Of course this provides value for the organisation, who amongst other things, will reap the rewards of enhanced capacity management and remove the complexity of performing this activity for them. This section will not labour on these examples as most standard marketing texts examine the ways in which the marketing mix can be manipulated to create value to satisfy identified market needs and wants. Likewise the strategy literature will also provide insight into the ways organisations seek to create value. For example, Michael Porter's (1980) work on the value chain and generic strategies are quite instructive in this regard. To aid understanding in this area you may wish to select an organisation, product, service

5

or campaign of interest and evaluate:

1 The value that is being offered the consumer

2 The ways in which the organisation is seeking to create this value.

In more recent conceptualisations, consumption is being conceived differently. In the marketing literature for example, the theory of 'service dominant logic' (SDL) Vargo and Lusch (2004, 2008a, 2008b) has been introduced that offers a new interpretation and explanation. Although providing a new lens for the whole marketing process, in the interest of this analysis, SDL specifically offers insight into new forms of consumption, but has not been fully embraced within experiences marketing as Williams states:

> Experiential marketing has become a cornerstone of many recent advances in areas such as retailing, branding and events marketing, however, marketing in the tourism and hospitality sectors does not appear to explicitly engaged the theoretical issues involved.

> (2006: 482)

Under the old dominant logic, marketing is transaction orientated; operations and resources are created and put to market by incumbent organisations to be acted upon by consumers. Consumers are thus conceived as the entities described above. They are merely the start and end point of market activity. Having identified their needs and wants, the targeted consumers are the ones the organisation creates value for. They are the ones who ultimately devour and absorb the value that is created for them. As an outcome of this process, the organisation is hopefully able to profit in some way, be it economically or otherwise from the transaction involved. In the new logic however, marketing is conceived as a dynamic process where the consumer has an active participative role in value creation. Rather than being the final destructive act of marketing transactions, within the theory of SDL, consumption is now thought of as an active dynamic process of ongoing value creation. Value is never static, finalised or complete. It is always in transition, always being (re)created. As a result, the definitions and terminology that traditionally circumscribe the of term 'consumer' and 'consumption' are now being re-thought and re-labelled. Having adopted and integrated producer behaviours into their consumption, utilizing portmanteau terms such as pro-sumer (e.g. Ritzer *et al.* 2012), and co-producer (Vargo and Lusch 2008a) now seem like more fitting descriptors.

Whilst these emergent theories have been introduced here, in the section devoted to actual consumption, they do relate to the other elements of the consumption cycle. Not only is value being refined, perpetuated, challenged and changed through the act of consumption, it is also unfolding through the processes of selection, acquisition and disposition (for discussion of values see Chapter 8). Kozinets (2002b) for example, has demonstrated the ways in which coffee aficionados create and share value between themselves on the alt.coffee online user group. By providing reviews, recommendations and critiques of products and methods of preparation and consumption of coffee, this community provides an active and dynamic resource for its members, which not only enhances the experience of consuming coffee, it also aids selection and purchasing through providing a informational source about a multitude of related products. Kozinets (1998, 2010) also provides a useful framework that describes the behaviour and roles played by consumers of online communities that is worth reading if this emerging area of consumption is of interest. We will return to examine and expand on these new forms of consumption later in this chapter.

■ Dispossession

Dispossession includes the numerous ways in which a consumer withdraws or removes themselves from a consumption experience or disposes of a product once it has served its purpose. As with all the previous elements of the cycle, this can be anything from a simple unconsidered act or a drawn out immersive process. So for example, having peeled an orange or eaten the contents of a bag of crisps, one could merely throw the peel or packet in the bin or alternatively place the peel in a compost heap for future consumption in the form of fertiliser, or seek to recycle the crisp packet. These behaviours may demonstrate and link to a consumer's values and interests and are therefore instructive acts in themselves with marketing value. Innocent drinks for example have expended much energy and time into the development and design of 100 per cent recyclable containers for its smoothie products (see http://www.innocentdrinks.co.uk/us/ethics/sustainable_packaging/). Not only does this meet the espoused environmental values of the company (for discussions of sustainable and green marketing see Chapter 10), these design innovations also provide additional value for the environmentally aware consumer and also a tangible competitive advantage for the company. Likewise the way in which a diner leaves a restaurant may be similarly instructive, leaving a tip and kind words as opposed to an abrupt and rushed conclusion to a meal may provide insight into a consumer's thoughts and perceptions. Although in most cases of consumption the consumer does move through some form of dispossession act or process, emergent marketing theory advocates a continual relationship. In exiting a consumption event such as a holiday or festival the consumer is left with memories and artefacts (often souvenirs or photographs) that will serve to inform future decisions thus closing the loop of the consumption cycle. Importantly, marketers of service orientated business, who do not fully benefit from the tangible reminders of physical products, should take great care in the memories that are left with consumers. The consumption process is an individual journey for the consumer, each person find different meanings, means of choosing, acquiring, consuming and disposing of the experiences within the consumption of tourism, hospitality, events and food. This relationship is partly formed by the fact that we are individual with a different life biography that will inform and direct the process. As each consumer will relate to the consumption process differently, it is important that we have the ability to define and locate our customers. The next section explores this area of interest in some depth.

Locating the consumer

Without wanting to present, or overplay a reductionist thesis, it is not unreasonable to claim that many marketing texts and practitioners treat consumers as a target. Whilst the professional guiding frameworks of both the CIM and AMA acknowledge the consumer's role and apparent power in the marketing process, when it comes down to it most books treat them as an entity with needs to be identified, anticipated and satisfied through the market offer. Whilst this approach may have practical utility it does not allow for the nuance and challenges that contemporary consumers present to marketers. This section seeks to address this dilemma by providing a more thorough account of the consumer and marketplace behaviour.

Market segmentation: making consumers known

The concept, practice, and process of market segmentation, is the received view by which marketing practitioners make their customer known. Building on the premise that most, if not all, contemporary markets are characterised by consumer heterogeneity, that is, consumers demonstrate great plurality and diversity in their personal characteristics, traits, behaviours, desires, wants and needs, the segmentation technology seeks to cut through this clutter and confusion. Essentially market segmentation seeks to identify groups of consumers who share similar consumption needs and goals and then profile and classify them based on a combination and mixture of behavioural and personal characteristics. That is these characteristics structure consumption behaviour, characteristics that are usually drawn upon include demographic, socio-economic, geographic, psychographic, personality and life-style factors (McDonald and Dunbar 2010). Market segmentation has actually become an industry in its own right with organisations emerging and developing products that provides their own methodologies and tailored solutions. Examples of these include amongst others, ACORN, MOSAIC and VALS2. These traditional approaches to segmentation make the assumption that there is a fixed and deterministic relationship between a consumer and their consumption behaviour.

The danger of adopting an approach to segmentation that is dominated and informed by a singular deterministic approach is that it ignores the fact the consumer is an individual with individual tastes, needs and desires. What we argue is that a quantitative approach to segmentation provides the foundation and recognition of the market, but in order to develop effective marketing strategies within THEF, this traditional approach needs to be augmented with an approach that located the consumer at the centre of the process. It is also important to recognise that the consumer is a dynamic entity who will change perceptions and consumption patterns throughout their lives. An interesting theme is to assess the various definitions of age upon our consumption influences. Some of these categories include the following.

■ Age as segment

■ The old but cognitively young

In their study of 'thirty something' ravers, Goulding and Shankar (2004) provide ample evidence of chronological age being a problematic if not largely unsuitable basis for market segmentation. Drawing extensively on the work of Barak (e.g. 1985) their research aligns with his core thesis that age is both a cognitive and behavioural manifestation and a multidimensional construct. Rather than being a concept that reflects a range of differentiated and discreet periods of time relative to experience that are shared across the lifecycle of human beings, age is something that is deeply entwined in culture and to the lived experience and activity of consumers. People have different ages that significantly differ from their actual age based upon their year of birth (Goldsmith and Heiens 1992). Hence we have 'look age', 'do age', 'interest age', 'age as a reflection of group referral' and felt age'.

■ Look age

'Look age' refers to the age that a person looks. The notion here is that age related 'looks' can be appropriated and achieved through stylising, grooming practices, and assembling the right symbolic materials and resources. In Goulding and Shankar's (2004) account we have evidence of research informants who take conscious steps to preserve youthful appearance through engaging in dietary and exercise regimes, spending small fortunes on 'proclaimed' age retardant cosmetics, and to express it and fit in, through wearing 'rave' specific clothes and brands that are perceived to align with rave and dance culture. Look age can have a significant impact upon the type of THEF activities the individual engages in, for example the older surfer who expresses their look age and feel through their emergence in the surf culture, clothing etc.

■ Do age

What one does in relation to the range of leisure activities a person engages in underscore the concept of 'do age'. In general terms and in normal accounts of marketing and consumption a consensus exists as to what are considered to be the activities and pursuits of the young and those of the elderly. Given a continuum from very young to very old you could plot the fit between a broad range of activities and the general age profile of consumers. This is often at the expense of older consumers who seemingly are disproportionally neglected in relation to younger consumers in terms of product focus, innovation, and advertising (Szmigin and Carrigan 2001, 2000;

Carrigan and Szmigin 2000) However, outside marketing practice, in new accounts of consumption, the boundaries and structures that frame this relationship are becoming increasingly blurred and fragmented. No more so than in Goulding and Shankar's (2004) account of ravers and raving. Seemingly, the rave provides the consumer with an experiential escape hatch from other normative structures and expectations that frame their lived experience of age such as doing 'grown up' work or having serious responsibilities that are linked to chronological age and accumulated work experience and knowledge. In their study, most of the informants represented the professional middle class, including management consultants, academics, and company directors. In this respect the rave, and other similar forms of activity provide the platform and context for older consumers to experience youth through doing the activities of the young and performing youth, have incredible potential for postmodern forms of liberation and emancipation (Firat and Venkatesh 1995) such as having the freedom to be whatever age one wants to be. The paradox here however is that for an activity to make someone older feel qualitatively younger then it still must have relevance and identification with the young or more youthful. Here lies a significant marketing problem and challenge, how do you attract older consumers to activities and experiences of the young without destroying the foundations upon which the experience is legitimised, and without alienating the consumers you trying to engage and attract.

■ Interest age

We next have a related concept, 'interest age'. As in the example above, this concept is dependent upon the notion of there being a set of definable and identifiable interests that have some correlation or relationship with specific age cohorts and activities. Thus the idea here is that subjective age is located in the set of interests that one has, engages, and finds enjoyment in. In the case of the cognitively young raver this includes cultivating knowledge, and maintaining interest in, DJs, music styles and genres, having an interest in the associated fashion and styles and by following the trends and reportage through publications such as *Mixmag* and *DJ* magazines. Equally to identify as a 'true' participant and practitioner one must also be conversant with the development and roots of the scene. Namely that it developed from early roots in Chicago and Detroit and in the early Balearic sound of Ibiza, hitting the UK in clubs like Shoom and Spectrum in the late 1980s having being imported by British pioneers who had holidayed on the 'White Isle' (Goulding and Shankar 2004; Goulding *et al.* 2009).

■ Age as a reflection of group referral

Age as a reflection of group referral acknowledges that 'age identity... *is*... confirmed through interaction with similar others' (Goulding and Shankar 2004: 647 emphasis added). In the case of the raver then, finding sociality and acceptance in the community of likeminded others, that is to say, group membership is central to age identification, even if these groups are ephemeral and located in distinct times, places and spaces, such as 'in the club' or during .the weekend'. Equally it is also argued that age is also experienced and validated through being able to identify with those that are perceived to be like oneself but also through being able to disassociate from those who are not. In this sense, age is related to social comparison, social positioning and through alignment and differentiation with the wider social body and politic. Barack et al. (2001) for example argues that Cher, Arnold Schwarzenegger, Tina Turner and Clint Eastwood model and embody lifestyles, virtues and values that are located across the younger age spectrum, and provide support, codes of behaviour and legitimise the pursuit for younger, fuller, more vigorous and glamorous lives. An interesting current case in point is the recent Saga cruises commercial (2012) which offers the older consumer a route and entry into a playful, vibrant and youthful life. To the tune of Tony Bennett's (1962) 'I'm just a lucky so and so', the third age is glamorised and idealised

5

through being staged and acted out in chauffeured Mercedes limousines, and then by youthful and good looking *'grey consumers'* (Carrigan 1998; Goulding 1999) taking mid-evening canapés with champagne, on board the deck of a luxury cruise ship, while wearing evening dresses and dinner jackets against the backdrop of a beautiful orange and purple sunset. In this sense people seek out, and find comfort in those that are 'just like me'.

■ Felt age

Finally we have felt age which denotes the difference between a person's chronological age and how old they actually feel. In many respects this is inextricably linked to the other dimensions of age that we review here. This is in the sense that how you look, what you do, your collective interests, how others perceive you, and how you position yourself relative to others, all have an influence and bearing on the age you feel. Equally physical state and condition is a determinate. Indeed as Barak et al. (2001) infer, given global trends in keeping fit, healthy dietary behaviour and related growth in access to preventative medical care, medicine and education, it is probable that as one ages, the gulf between felt age and chronological age widens. Thus, opening up ever more markets for the old but cognitively young, for example, the rise in medical and cosmetic tourism as a distinctive niche (see Tresidder 2011b). In making this argument however it is prudent to reflect on the notion that this concept does not necessarily work one way. Indeed in closing their paper Goulding and Shankar (2004) point out that the fit between chronological and cognitive age may also be fractured and unsynchronised within the young and teenage age cohorts as well. The young may be as equally compelled to experience and act out being older as much as the old are younger. The identification of age as a means of segmentation is a good example of how the deterministic approach to market segmentation is found wanting.

■ Personality as segment

Chapter 6 explores how our consumption patterns become a social marker of who we are, however we can also make the claim that out consumption patterns also reflect our personality (Kassarjian 1971). The adoption of a more qualitative approach to understanding consumers enables one to understand the individual consumer's wants, desires and needs. Thus the food we eat, the destinations or events we visit are a direct extension of individual preferences and personality traits. Carducci (2009) explores personality by examining interpersonal coping strategies by adapting Horney's (1945) CAD approach and can be utilised in marketing to create a marketing approach that meets the need of the individual and is reflected in the choice of products, activities, experiences, images, words and communication themes and channels chosen. CAD in the context of experiences marketing may be defined as:

C   Measures interpersonal style of moving towards others, or in other words, people who fall into this category generally want to be accepted and loved by others. This in terms of experiences marketing can be seen as the largest group of consumers and generally want to be seen as part of the mass market where to be part of the collective reinforces the experience of leisure/tourism etc. Often safety and security will be found through the consumption of mass or established experiences in which all of the consumers/customers become part of a consumption group, and will lead to some form of communitas. This group are attracted by the THEF marketing campaigns that focus on families, being part of groups, being loved.

A   Personalities that move against people, people with these traits have the tendency to compete and have a desire to win. This manifests itself in a more individualistic experience which is competitive physically (adventure based experiences), sexually (Hedonism II) or even culturally (painting holidays)) and kudos come from the consumption of the product. This is often in direct opposition to family-focused marketing that revolves around safety, familiarity and security.

D   Personalities that move away from people or more simplistically individuals who desire independence and freedom from obligation. Consumers with these personality traits have no particular preferences and are more likely to engage with tourism, hospitality, events or food in a more individualistic and independent manner. These consumers will often book their own tours, flights, hotels etc. and will often define themselves as travellers rather than tourists, will search for locally owned non-chain accommodation, will search for events that reflect this trait.

It is also possible to take the profiling of consumer's personality traits a step further by attempting to understand how they assign value to goods and services. This can be seen as a direct reflection of their personality and defines the consumer's relationship to the products we are attempting to sell, by adopting certain consumption patterns and as such the approach to marketing differs by targeting each of them in differing ways. Consumers can be broadly categorised into three broad behavioural groups:

■ Consumers motivated by materialism

Consumers have differing relations to products and goods, some consumers are more motivated to buy and purchase goods as a means of expressing their identity and position in society through consumption. Thus, the way in which experiences marketing sell or offers a lifestyle appeals directly to the materialistically motivated consumers (Belk 1985). For example, food retailers will make their food adverts aspirational, by elevating the food in the advert to that of sophisticated dining even when in reality they are selling a microwavable ready meal. Events, holiday and restaurants offer a glimpse of a lifestyle that is often beyond the reach of the ordinary consumer, but is achievable during a holiday or as a marker of a special event within their lives.

■ Consumers with fixed consumption patterns

Often consumers will build a relationship with a product or service that is underpinned by trust (Morgan and Hunt 1994), and as a result will only purchase that good or service. Often consumers will eat at the same restaurant or visit the same destination and stay in the same hotel for a number of years. In terms of marketing practice this type of fixed behaviour is easy to manage for those companies or organisation that already has the relationship with the consumer, but is more difficult for competitors to entice consumers to try new products or experiences (Rook 1985). Thus, for the restaurant that already has a strong relationship with its customers which has resulted in fixed consumption patterns then, the marketing will revolve around reinforcing this relationship by offering loyalty schemes etc. A new restaurant however, may have to try out-manoeuvre competitors by undermining the product, service or experience, or offer incentive schemes that may tempt new customers or to break fixed consumption patterns.

■ Consumers with compulsive behaviour patterns

Supermarkets have recognised for many years that many of their customers have compulsive behaviour patterns and have designed and structured their stores to encourage this behaviour. Initiatives such as 'buy on get one free', free credits offers or locating sweets at the checkout till all encourage consumers to purchase items they did not plan to buy. These consumers do not think about the consequence of their purchasing patterns and are easily persuaded (Rook 1987; O'Guinn and Faber 1989), thus campaigns will focus around conventions such as 'once in a lifetime opportunity' or 'buy two weeks and get the third free' etc.

THEF marketing is not just a physical process, but is also a psychological one, the intangible nature of events, tourism, hospitality and food, requires experiences marketers to utilise a very specific language of marketing (as seen in Chapter 8) that appeals to the senses, imagination and personality of the consumer. By understanding the various traits, and elements of the individual's personality it is possible to enhance marketing by segmentation to create an approach that targets the traits of consumers and will ultimately lead to an enhanced relationship between the product and the consumer (Belk 1985; Marsden and Littler 1998). However, one of the most significant aspects of experiences marketing is that tourism, hospitality, events and food are fundamentally concerned with searching for and finding various forms of pleasure or fun. It is argued that humans are 'pleasure seekers' and are predisposed to search for fun (O'Shaughnessy and O'Shaughnessy 2002), as such we are all hedonistic beings and this makes up a part of our psychology and personality.

■ Hedonism and THEF marketing

THEF marketing provides access into a world that is dominated by fun or hedonism, each consumer will define fun or search for fun in differing ways. Thus in order to understand the needs of the consumer and how they consume THEF, we need to explore notions of hedonistic or ludic behaviour. Hedonistic or ludic behaviour (see Kozinets et al 2004) has always been a central precept of THEF (Cohen 1995) in the form of festivals and carnivals, the act of celebration has been a significant element of our lives. As stated in Chapter 2, it makes sense of our lives and justifies our existence. Krippendorf (1999) goes as far as to state that tourism is a form of social therapy, and that its consumption revitalises and soothes us. Thus, in order to understand how consumers relate to experiences marketing, it is important that we examine the notion of hedonism and how we find pleasure as this informs how companies or organisations theme or structure their products, services, activities and campaigns. It is also important to recognise that each of us creates our own pleasure zones, and as such we create and construct an environment that enables us to gain the maximum levels of pleasure possible.

What we find pleasurable is a direct reflection of our personalities and worldview, however experiences marketing is adept at creating campaigns that create liminal spaces in which we may locate our desires, while the industry creates products and services that meet our desires. For example we can see the delivered pizza as creating an aesthetic of consumption that creates pleasure and gratification. Thus rather than going through the process of utilitarian shopping (as opposed to hedonistic shopping) where we buy ingredients, go home, to make the pizza, which leaves us with a mess and washing up. On top of this we have to wait to experience the meal, where the alternative is to order over the phone, the pizza is made for us, we have unlimited choice as to the toppings, there are lots of extras that heighten the experience, we can choose dips, drinks, deserts. It is then delivered to us. The 'ideal pizza', a pizza that has been made especially for us, it is bespoke, made by experts, no one else will have a pizza like ours, it is the best pizza in the world. The experience of eating, of ordering a pizza become elevated to a hedonistic aesthetic that underpins the concept of experiences marketing. However, if the consumer does not like pizza, it would not be a pleasurable experience for them, also the notion of hedonism is formed in many ways, so people find pleasure in many differing experiences. In order to understand how the individual finds pleasure Schiffman and Kanuk (2007) identify four forms of hedonism that are particularly significant for experiences marketing.

■ Psychological hedonism

This may be defined as the most dominant definition of hedonism as it reflects the fact that we all naturally seek pleasure. This category underpins the majority of experiences marketing, whereby campaigns focus on the fun, pleasure element of the experience.

■ Moral or ethical hedonism

It has been recognised by marketers (O'Shaughnessy and O'Shaughnessy 2002), for a considerable time that consumers are attracted to ethical products and campaigns. There is pleasure in knowing that we have caused no damage or are making an ethical choice. Many companies and organisation have invested in marketing their green or ethical credentials. Companies such as Cadbury's and Starbucks have adopted a 'Fairtrade' approach through their production and purchasing strategies, as a result of this a number of their recent marketing campaigns have focused on this rather than the product. Holiday companies such as Center Parcs have always made their environmental policy a central premise of their promotion strategy, while events such as Glastonbury donate profits to Greenpeace. The inclusion of a moral theme adds capital to the product and removes some of the barriers to consumption by enabling consumers to obtain pleasure from their ethical behaviour.

■ Universal hedonism

This approach makes the assumption that there is a human right to have access to things that provide pleasure (O'Shaughnessy and O'Shaughnessy 2002). Thus, there is a pleasure in undertaking activities as part of a group who are also finding pleasure. This very much underpins the notion of being part of a group, audience or mass all sharing and expecting the same experiences. This is experiences in the communitas which accompanies festivals, carnivals and tourism.

■ Rationalising hedonism

The concept of rational recreation is not a new one, the rationalisation of leisure was used in the mid-19th century to create a better educated and healthier workforce (Clarke and Critcher 1985). There is a pleasure in feeling that you are bettering yourself through activity, this can include gaining pleasure from educational, spiritual, cultural or physically-based activities. Such activities are often removed from traditional experiences of eating, drinking and sun-bathing associated with traditional holiday. The idea of abstinence or getting healthier underpins many aspects of experiences marketing and although it may be seen to be in opposition to the more dominant definitions of hedonism, abstinence can still be seen as a hedonistic activity for some consumers (Cole 2008).

Thus, each consumer group or individual will search for the things that given them most pleasure and the choices they make in booking their holiday, hotel or tickets for an event reflects this choice. Kahnx, Ratner and Kanemen sum up this process perfectly:

> Consider how a consumer decides which songs to play at a jukebox. If only one song is going to be played, the decision is easy: choose the song that brings the most enjoyment.
>
> (1997: 85)

Thus consumer choice will reflect the experience they believe is going to give them the most pleasure for the limited amount of money and time they possess. As such, the language of THEF as discussed in Chapter 8 represents not only a semiotic language, but also a hedonic discourse of experiences marketing. Jin et al (2003) illustrate how such a hedonic discourse can inform even the simple activity of shopping, they state that there are two different types of shopping (as alluded to earlier in this chapter).

- **Utilitarian shopping** includes the majority of shopping activities such as purchasing the items we need to exist (in other words this may be seen to fall into the profane category). It is part of the ordinary, the mundane; as such it lacks the excitement of hedonic shopping and thus lacks pleasure.

- **Hedonic shopping** makes up the element of shopping that excites, the search for bargains, luxury items or those special things that we reward ourselves with. This is in direct opposition to utilitarian shopping. (This type of activity clearly falls into the sacred category of activities.)

We can also use this distinction to understand how the level of pleasure or hedonism will differ according to the context and purpose of the activity. For example, the degree of pleasure attending an event will depend upon the motivation, the purpose of travel, and eating to live, for business or celebration will all determine individual pleasure levels. It is interesting to note that the production of marketing strategies and contexts recognise these boundaries and identifies that often there is a blurring between the utilitarian and the hedonic. A good example of this is incentivised travel whereby there is an assumption that travel will increase productivity.

The blurring of boundaries between work and pleasure is a popular convention in experiences marketing. If the business element is being marketed then the materials will also often contain links back to the facility to give you pleasure once your work is completed, for example the fine dining restaurants, the spa facilities, the nightlife of the destination. This approach attempts to reconcile the hedonistic needs of the individual consumer. Marketing can be seen to induce the need for and create expectations around hedonic consumption patterns.

◼ Vicarious hedonism

The purpose of experiences marketing is to create interest or to sell our experience, however the pleasure of consumption starts not when we physically consume the product, but commences when we start to plan, compare, research and engage in the marketing communication process. This element builds anticipation, it enables us to begin the journey before we have left home, Solomon *et al.* (2010) list a number of hedonistic motivations and these can easily be adapted in the context of experiences marketing.

◼ Anticipated hedonism

Pleasure is gained from the anticipated benefits or experiences you may gain from the actual consumption of the experience. The consumption of tourism, food, hospitality and events begins with the anticipation, the thought of experience and the pleasure this may bring. Thus, THEF marketing offers a gateway into the world of anticipated pleasure and escape.

Role enactment

The consumption of experiences can be seen to change the status of the consumer and they become labelled as tourist, diner, guest etc. This change in status alters the social standing and position of the consumer, and this involves people adopting different roles. For example diners in a restaurant become the people being served; there is a shift in the power relations of that individual as they are in control of the service encounter. Additionally by attending a music event we are released from our normal social constraints, this enables us to behave in a different way to our usual behaviour. The adoption of the role as an experience consumer is informed by a hedonic discourse that enables us to escape from the pressures of everyday life and enter into a time and space that allows us to explore other identities.

Choice optimisation

Researching the experience and examining the offers and deals available, feeling that you have managed to track down and purchase the best buy also creates a hedonistic response. This probably explains the growth and enthusiastic response of consumers to discount voucher sites such as Wowcher and social media sites such as Laterooms.com and Lastminute.com.

Negotiation

Bartering and negotiation for goods and services is often a central experience of being a tourist, the ability to negotiate the price of the service or experience also provides pleasure and satisfaction. Supermarkets remove this bartering element and pacify the consumer interaction, thus removing a pleasurable element of the shopping process for many people.

■ Affiliation

One of the central aspects as defined in Chapter 6, is the idea that we are part of a crowd that is experiencing the same experience. This leads to feelings of belonging and possessing a shared cultural capital or even habitus, in the service encounter this is expressed in the feeling of communitas we find through the consumption of tourism, hospitality, events and food.

■ Power and authority

This is closely related to the role enactment and the persona we adopt as consumers. The feeling of controlling the service relationship, of having power over someone raises feelings of self esteem and position in society and thus generating a form of pleasure underpinned by perceived superiority. It is interesting to note that much research has been undertaken (see Dann 1996a; Tresidder 2010a) on the representation of local people in tourism brochures and in the large majority of cases they are presented as either attractions or providing service, this convention forms a significant discourse in tourism and hospitality marketing. This theme is explored further in Chapter 8.

■ Stimulation

Experiences marketing utilises the concept of escape, adventure and excitement as one of its core themes, this often offers experiences that are opposite to the routine orientated structure of everyday life. What is being offered within such promotion is the opportunity to enter into an extraordinary world of experiences that remove us from everyday life; the search for new and interesting experiences is a significant element in the language of tourism, hospitality, events and food and forms part of the hedonic discourse of experiences marketing.

All of the above form a discourse that moves away from emotions and focuses on the sensations we may encounter as tourists, guests or as a part or an audience. THEF marketing utilises marketing communications to create a sensual world that is vicariously consumed as pre-physical consumption. However the pleasure element starts at the initial marketing/promotion stage and becomes elevated as we get nearer to actual consumption.

■ Conclusion

This chapter has provided an introduction into defining the consumer and briefly examined some of their motivational factors. This chapter only touches on a small number of consumption influence and determinants. It has also located the consumer within a process that relates to the activities that are integral to the consumption of THEF experiences, consumers need to select, purchase, consume their THEF experience. The way in with the consumer relates to THEF experiences is central to understanding both their motivations and how as marketers we define and target the potential consumer. It is important that we attempt to understand how preferences are formed and how the consumption process differs from individual to individual. Tourists, diners or guests are not just a statistic or part of a trend, but are complex free-thinking entities that need to be understood and located within a holistic marketing environment. Consumption and the values we attribute to the product or experience form a significant element of the interaction and communication between producer and consumer, the next chapter examines how both consumer and society utilise consumption practices to express identity and reinforce their membership within particular consumption groups or tribes.

6 Habitus, Distinction, Identity and Cultural Capital

■ Introduction

This book revolves around two assumptions, the first is that marketing is a cultural activity that is both informed and part of contemporary culture and that secondly that marketing needs to understand the relationship between the individual consumer and the product or experience. This chapter outlines the significance of consumption and how we use our consumption patterns to both reinforce our identity and position within society. This chapter also challenges the dominance of certain marketing practices such as segmentation in targeting consumers. We all think carefully before we purchase something whether it be a holiday or a meal, we go through a complex decision-making process taking into account many different factors, one of the major aspects will be to think about what additional benefits will we get from purchasing the item: 'What will my family, friends or even strangers think?'. As such, we try to identify the additional benefits from purchasing the item, for example if I buy a designer coat I will get the benefit of being kept warm, but also I will get the benefit of people thinking I am affluent and trendy, and as such they may look up to me or give me respect. This process also informs the things we drink, the places we holiday at, the events we attend, the wine we choose or the restaurants we eat at, it can be argued that we go through this process every time we purchase an item or experience. Consumption identifies to the rest of the world the type of person we are and identifies the groups, class or tribe we belong to. This chapter examines how we reinforce or create our identity through consumption, how and why we join consumption groups and the impact this may have on contemporary marketing practices.

■ The restructuring of society and the consumer

As we moved from an economy dominated by industrial production to one dominated by services and experiences, such as banking, insurance, entertainment and even events, hospitality, catering and tourism or in other words from industrialisation to post-industrialisation, both culture and society adapted with it. The changes in working patterns, the destruction of regionally dominant industries such as coal mining or steel production saw the breakdown of communities and increased migration by workers looking to access the new service industries. This is significant for a number of reasons, firstly the community groups that help us form our identities and informed our view of the world disappeared and was replaced by a more powerful and persuasive media that generated ways of living through cable or satellite television, or the freedom of information that accompanied the Internet. What we have witnessed is a restructuring of society in which workers have become consumers and as such a society that is dominated by consumerism and has led to a world in which:

> ...the meaning of life is to be found in buying things and repackaging experiences supplanting 'religion', work, and politics as the mechanism by which social and status distinctions may be established.
>
> (Izberk-Bilgin 2010: 302)

6

This is a world in which 'cultural intermediaries' specifically in advertising, the media, the fashion system, product development, broadcasting and entertainment act as social and cultural brokers (Urry 2001), they define the way in which we view the world, by defining taste, trends and fashions. This group of individuals and their organisations have replaced traditional family and kinship groups in defining our expectations and desires. However, it should not be forgotten that throughout history certain consumption patterns have always supported social class (Holt 1998).

Magazines and television programmes that chart the lives of celebrities, by focusing on their lifestyles, their diets, their leisure time, their holidays, supported by travel programmes, advertisements and, how-to guides, create demand in THEF by providing subject positions, or blueprints to live through/by, and as a result, we may emulate the rich and famous or aspirant others. In short, cultural intermediaries are significantly active in the definition of taste and preferences, and in creating subject positions that are made available for consumers as resources through which they can activate and express or develop their identities. The result of this is that commodities are no longer solely defined by their function or use, or by their market price, but rather by what they signify to both the consumer and his or her peers (Izberk-Bilgin 2010; Levy 1959; Solomon 1983). Experiences marketing utilises the knowledge and symbolism generated by cultural intermediaries and the manifold meanings located in the broader culturally constituted world (McCracken 1986) to inform their own marketing practice and cultural intermediation. It enables the marketer to tailor and develop products, experiences, and mark out the boundaries of specific fields of consumption or habitus (Arsel and Thompson 2011) that offer the maximum benefits/value to the consumer by providing them with the means and resources to generate and accumulate various forms of capital, be it cultural, social, symbolic, or even economic (Thompson and Arsel 2004). Drawing on the myriad of symbolic and discursive resources, the language and practice of experiences marketing invites us into a plurality of worlds in which to accumulate capital, activate and furnish our identity projects, and the potential to escape from the mundane experience of everyday life, that is, if we are endowed with the financial and authoritative resources and capabilities (Arnould et al. 2006). Experiences marketing, defines taste and provides an outlet to express our own individual taste and preferences though the consumption of the experience.

■ Taste and consumption

The type of destination we visit, holiday, event, food or hotel we choose is a significant reflection of our own individual taste. However, taste is socially and culturally conditioned, while consumer choice reflects a 'symbolic hierarchy' (Allen and Anderson 1994: 70) that is defined and maintained by society. This hierarchy enables groups of consumers to distance or make themselves distinct from other individuals or groups by defining trends, consumption patterns or expressions of taste. Thus, the things we buy, drink, eat, drive, wear, the events we attend, the destinations or attractions we visit and the broader consumption practices we either engage in or disengage from, become a social marker of who we are, and increasingly becomes an integral aspect of our self-concept and a symbolic and social resource that has positional power within particular status hierarchies (see Levy 1959; Belk 2010 for review). As Allen and Anderson state:

> taste becomes a 'social weapon' that defines and marks off the high from the low, the sacred from the profane, and the 'legitimate' from the 'illegitimate'.

> (1994: 70)

Our consumption patterns as consumers represent who we are and much of the meaning and symbolic authority of products is generated through the marketing process. Marketing has the ability to elevate brands and logos from the ordinary to that of the extraordinary, one of the best ways to think about this is to locate

6

the debate within the field of designer clothes. For example, I can go to a high street store and purchase a very good quality polo shirt for £30, it is good cotton, it has nice buttons, however, I can also go to a store and purchase a polo shirt of the same quality as the £30 version, but because the shirt has an embroidered man on a horse I am willing to pay £80. Thus, the symbolic values of the logo is worth £50, value is generated through the sign and the symbolism of the logo. As a consumer I am willing to pay this additional amount, as the shirt comes to represent a way of living, a view of the world that is defined by perceived notions of sophistication, class and wealth. Thus, the shirt is not just a means to clothe myself, but also an expression of the type of person I am or at least want to be seen as. We each find meaning in the brand we purchase and there is clear evidence that consumers physically and symbolically transform branded goods as they coproduce collective, family and individual meanings (Holt 1998: 20). The marketing process is key to this as it creates and reinforces the meaning and significant of the logo or brand etc. This process also underpins experiences marketing.

Within experiences marketing we see knowledge and a cultural awareness being continually generated. We evaluate and make judgements about people through their knowledge of food, culture, wine, geography and how they express this through their consumer behaviour and consumption choices. If someone attends a classical concert we may make certain assumptions about that person, their education, cultural knowledge and social position, we make a different set of assumptions if someone attends a folk concert or the Ministry of Sound. We enter into the same process when we assess leisure activities or holiday choices and the activities they engage in during this time. We will make different judgements about people visiting the same destination but undertaking different activities, for example two tourists are on the same plane on route to Ibiza, one is there to visit the clubs and to see a particular DJ, the other is going to hike in the mountains and visit the churches in the hills.

Although the destination may be the same, both are expressing different forms of cultural capital, one is expressing their knowledge of the dance scene, the other the knowledge of ecclesiastical architecture in the Balearics. This expression of knowledge expresses who they are, which market segment they belong to, their membership to a particular class or group of people and their position within this group.

Cultural capital

Our choice of food, concert or holiday generates what may be termed cultural capital which is simply the additional social benefits we may gain from certain activities. We exchange our cultural capital with friends, family and peers and the amount of cultural capital we are judge to have by these groups will identify where we sit hierarchically within the social group. Our expression of cultural capital may cement our position, or it may place us in a position that people look up to and want to emulate. There are two types of capital, capital that is entwined with wealth and money, and cultural capital that is defined by types and levels of knowledge. For Holt (1998) the role of cultural capital in contemporary society attracts the respect of others and plays an important role in structuring consumption patterns. Simplistically, Cultural Capital consists of:

6

1   Cultural knowledge, skills, experiences, abilities

2   Linguistic competence and vocabulary

3   Modes of thought and views of the world (see Chapter 7 for discussion on this area).

We all possess particular levels of knowledge about different subjects and experiences and consumption patterns, this knowledge in conjunction with consumption forms our cultural capital, and this form of capital locates us within society or groups. Holt asserts that:

Cultural capital exists in three primary forms: embodied as practical knowledges, skills, and dispositions; objectified in cultural objects; and institutionalized in official degrees and diplomas that certify the existence of the embodied form.

(1998: 3)

Cultural capital is not merely an expression of elitist groups but is important in defining membership of cultural groupings, for example people will express their knowledge of football, the intricacies of the game, their historical knowledge of players and games etc. (see Richardson and Turley 2007 or Holt 1997 for discussion of American baseball and knowledge). This interest or knowledge is still a form of cultural capital that enables individuals to locate themselves within a group of people that share the same interests and worldview that may be termed a shared 'capital space'. As Bourdieu states, members of this will '...have every chance of having similar dispositions and interests, and thus producing similar practices and adopting similar stances' (1981: 231). Thus, for marketers, understanding the various habitus and the needs and desires of its members provides an effective method of segmenting and constructing communication strategies that are shaped through various cultural understandings etc. It is of particular significance to experiences marketing as tourism, hospitality, events and food play a central role in people expressing their levels of cultural capital and adding to it.

■ Cultural capital and taste

Cultural capital as defined by Pierre Bourdieu represents a distinct competitive resource that people concurrently possess, embody and accumulate. As previously described, it takes the form of knowledge, skills, aptitude, and abilities which are transcribed in consumer tastes and consumption practices. These in turn become resources that are deployed for both autotelic and instrumental reasons (Holt 1997). For example, with regard to the latter, cultural knowledge and skill could be deployed as an interpretive framework and set of associated practices to appreciate the idiosyncratic qualities of cheese or a micro brewed beer. That is, it is activated in the service of connoisseurship; for personal pleasure and enjoyment. Alternatively, cultural capital may be explicitly groomed and deployed in pursuit of status, recognition or group membership. Objectified cultural capital that is manifest through observable or recognised consumption practices may grant a consumer access to esteemed or distinct social networks or communities. Conversely, deficiencies in capital could also produce the opposite effects by diminishing a consumers' relative status within a field, which in turn may exclude them from that field and from social relationships. To this end, objectified cultural capital delineates and marks out symbolic and semiotic boundaries that have significant social (and economic) significance (Holt 1997), or to put it another way, cultural capital translates into social capital. While this suggests that a consumer may always be purposively working their cultural capital for explicit personal benefit, this is not always the case.

It is worth noting that in many cases this resource is at work socially, without it being recognised personally by a consumer. For certain consumers their social positioning, community affiliation and group membership is just the way things are. That is, it is acting to position them within a certain social strata or group without their explicit knowledge and indirectly becomes a means of distinction and criteria for selection to esteemed or affiliate networks and groups. In this respect, as with economic capital , cultural capital can be understood as a mediator between person, experience and opportunity. That is to say, the specific quantity and quality of capital a person possesses delimits their potential as a consumer across and within the range of specific and generic 'fields' of consumption. Like Holt (1998), and Arsel and Thompson (2011), we use the Bourdieuian concept of 'field' to represent the range of consumer goods, activities and experiences that constitute consumer society and include experiences or services. While Bourdieu used the term 'field' to classify and distinguish between the religion,

6

politics, economic and consumption. In respect of this book, the field would encompass both the sectors themselves, namely the fields of THEF, and also the 'sub-fields' that reside within those sectors, such as: the fine dining field; the adventure tourism field; the cultural events field; the field of coffee; the barbecue field, and so forth and as such directly impact upon consumption patterns and buyer behaviour.

Consumers buying behaviour or consumption pattern become a tripartite-interrelated process:

1   It is needed to engage successfully in a consumption activity – for example the skills needed to perform the necessary symbolic act are needed for entry into the clubs, or skills of extreme self to survive the harsh conditions of the desert of the Burning Man festival.

2   It adds to their particular stock of cultural capital, for example wearing an 'I survived the Burning Man festival' tee shirt offers a direct expression of the wearer's cultural capital.

3   It simultaneously expresses their cultural capital endowments. Thus, I go to a particular, club, destination, restaurant or event because I have knowledge of it, thus the knowledge of the experience is an expression of my cultural capital and then by attending/consuming the experience I am adding to my bank cultural capital.

This capital will be later used as a means of distinction from other consumers or reinforcing membership to a group or class. This view is supported by Holt in his 1998 work where he identifies a number of themes, interests and activities that are closely associated with consumption, identity and cultural capital; these include *Exoticism, Authenticity, Cosmopolitanism,* and *Connoisseurship.* All of these categories are closely allied to THEF, and as such the consumption of experiences is a major means by which the individual may express both their identity and cultural capital, in short leisure becomes a tool for self-actualisation (Holt 1998: 17). Experiences marketing often utilises a language that reinforces the cultural significance of the activity, this providing a consumption outlet for the expression of your status, class and habitus.

■ Habitus as market segment

The ability to recognise how consumers construct their identity, the dynamics of particular habitus and the trends or themes that cultural intermediaries are generating are key to contemporary marketing strategy. The ability to understand the interrelationship between these various aspects of the production and consumption process provides an insight into the type of products that need to be developed, the semiotic language that should be used and the most appropriate communication channels for each group, habitus or tribe. This provides marketers with a competitive advantage as they are able to anticipate trends, and the needs and desires of particular consumers and to identify types of cultural capital that need to be exchanged with different groups. It is argued that we live in a 'classless society' and that the longstanding means of differentiating society into social groups dominated by the ruling elite no longer apply. This approach was widely adopted in traditional marketing approaches and is manifested in the 'ABC1' social class demographic and a means of defining or targeting consumers. However, during the era of postmodernity this means of differentiating consumers has been challenged and replaced by a more fluid egalitarian understanding of society and the consumer. Bourdieu identified that society was structured by individual cultural practices and preferences that were also shared by a group of peers, and went onto refer to these groups as forming a 'habitus'. Thus:

> One's class origin is not, therefore, a structural straight jacket that determines with certainty one's actions. But on the other hand, there is a certain probability that persons exposed to similar life experiences will display similar 'lifestyles'.
>
> (Allen and Anderson 1994: 71)

Individual consumption patterns become a means to define both yourself and your position in society or within a habitus (Henry and Caudwell 2008). Habitus becomes a complex system of distinctions based on constellations of taste (or according to Baudrillard (1998: 60) a 'social logic of consumption') that becomes a group-distinctive framework of social cognition and interpretation and which create communities of a particular lifestyle (Izberk-Bilgin 2010). For Miles:

> ...the 'habitus' is the embodiment of the cultural dispositions and sensibilities of the group that structure group behavior, simultaneously allowing group members a mechanism for structuring their social experience.
>
> (1996: 152)

This position is reinforced by the consumer's 'special knowledge of things' (ibid.). Within this context, any goods or activities may be used as a means of maintaining in-group solidarity and excluding status inferiors (Holt 1998).

Cultural and consumer knowledge is generated in many ways from television, to magazines, how-to books, family and peer interaction, and most importantly through PR and marketing activities. Consumers are surrounded by different forms and means of knowledge that is communicated. Our engagement and interaction with these various sources enables us to develop our cultural capital (Henry and Caudwell 2008), whether that information is concerning food choices, which bands to see, which destinations to visit or which hotel to stay in. Contemporary consumption patterns enable us to balance the need to express our individuality while finding the comfort of being able to belong to a group or tribe, micro culture (John Branch 2007), or community of consumption (see Cova and Cova 2006) that share consumption patterns, passion, emotion, values and knowledge. Cova and Cova (2002: 599) maintain that consumer tribes have the following characteristics:

- They are ephemeral and non-totalising groupings (they continually form and re-form according to trends and fashions).

- A person can belong to several tribes (people are complex and it is impossible to pigeon-hole individuals into a singular classification).

- The boundaries of the tribe are conceptual (members do not have to meet or even be in the same country to share membership).

- The members of the tribe are related by shared feelings and (re)appropriated signs (members share feelings about goods and experiences, and that knowledge is governed by a semiotic code of production and consumption [see Chapter 8 for full discussion of the semiotics of experiences marketing]).

Therefore, what we see is the emergence of new groups of consumers that have continually shifting relationships to fashion, trends and taste. This is reinforced by Cova and Cova who forward the assertion that:

6

> Of course, tribal groupings are not directly comparable with reference groups or psychographic segments. One the one hand, they differ from reference groups in that they do not focus on normative influences of the group or of individual group members on one another. Instead tribes concentrate on the bonding or linking element that keeps individuals in the group. Tribes differ from psychographic segments by their short life span and their diversity. It is fair to say that postmodern neo-tribalism translates a need to belong not to one but to several groups simultaneously, and that tribal membership does not involve set personality traits or same values, but expresses a shared experience of maybe only some aspects of a person's personal history.

> (2002: 602)

Rather than thinking of these groups or tribes as conventional segment groups that are defined by age, income, demographics etc. we need to think of individual consumers that form into identifiable groups through their relationship to culture and taste (Henry and Caudwell 2008). As Thompson and Troester (2002) state: 'These variegated subsystems of meaning cut across the master socio-logical categories such as gender, class, ethnicity, and age cohort.' Therefore, a habitus becomes '…a lens through which individuals interpret and categorize objects, people, and events' (Izberk-Bilgin 2010: 309). The practice of consuming THEF as represented in experiences marketing creates and forms consumption spaces in which groups or tribes can share and construct formulated social and cultural experiences and meanings. As membership comes from shared experience and meaning it is difficult to quantify membership, rather it needs to be thought of in terms of behavioural segmentation or interpretive similarity and as such qualitatively orientated. Within the realm of experiences marketing the love and shared semiotic resonance and significance of a band, destination, wine, food and luxury, transform individuals into an identifiable habitus and subsequent tribe.

The degree to which we adhere or immerse ourselves in a particular habitus or tribe is down to personal choice, and we may belong to more than one habitus, changing our identity according to social or cultural situations (Izberk-Bilgin 2010). For example, during the week an individual, as part of their work role, may adopt a professional and elitist approach to culture in order to fit in with their work and peers, this will result in the adoption of a particular work uniform such as a suit, language and expression of cultural knowledge such as exotic or traditional dining practices. At the weekend they may choose to go clubbing or surfing, this enables them to enter into another habitus with differing uniforms, language or consumption patterns and rituals etc. Thus, we choose the relationship, amount of interaction and membership type we have with an individual habitus, individuals can adopt one of four roles within a habitus or tribe, and these are:

- **An Adherent or Devotee:** Those individuals that are devoted to an activity, belong to organisations, clubs, attend specialist events etc.

- **A Participant:** Those individuals who participate and are very interested in the activity, but it is not their major interest or activity.

- **A Practitioner:** An individual who has daily involvement with the activity, a chef, events organiser or travel rep.

- **A Sympathiser:** An individual who is interested in the activity, but is free floating and only follows the activity as it is trendy and will move onto another activity once its significance is superseded.

(Adapted from Cova and Cova 2001: 71)

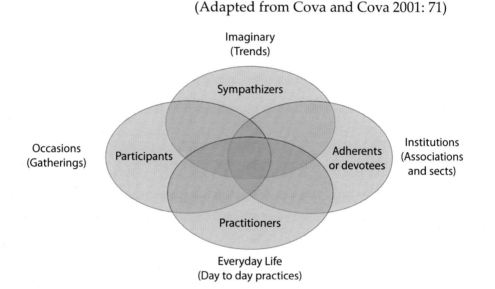

Figure 6.1: Role of Tribe Members (Cova and Cova 2002: 607)

The model in Figure 6.1 identifies the various roles we take within a tribe or habitus, and additionally identifies the hierarchies that exist within a habitus. The significance of this for marketers is that by understanding the dynamics of a habitus and the different members it is possible to develop a coherent marketing campaign that is tailored to meet the needs, desires and levels of cultural knowledge of its members. Tribal marketing thus needs to focus on the products, activities, experiences, and practices that hold people together by creating a 'we-ness'.

■ The role of cultural capital in organising taste and consumption practices

To further explain the operative effects of cultural capital and its capacity as a consumer resource we can further draw upon the work of Holt (1997, 1998) who has examined how quotas of cultural capital mediate the experiences and potential of American consumers. Specifically his research aimed to examine if consumption still served to reproduce social boundaries and class. His findings are instructive in terms of the ways in which cultural capital inflects the consumption of food and hospitality products and services. He constructed a measurement scale that allowed him to distinguish between consumers with high cultural capital resources (HCCs) and those with low (LCCs). To identify these typologies Holt drew reference from Bourdieu who holds that cultural capital endowments are both relative to, and accumulated through a person's formative socialisation by parenting and associated experiences; informal and formal education, and; acculturation processes and interactions that span one's work life and leisure experiences. Accordingly, those born to families who have highly educated parents who have experienced a cosmopolitan lifestyle through work, leisure and habitation, who then, themselves proceed on similar life trajectories by attending prestigious schools and elite universities and who following secure careers in professions that both emphasise symbolic production and knowledge or creative work and position them within a world that is replete with travel and metropolitan life, are on aggregate, going to exhibit and embody higher stocks of capital than those who do not. The logic of this arguments stems from the notion that such life trajectories produce privileged consumers/citizens that will have developed through their socialisation, training, work and leisure experiences the capacity for critical abstract thought, accumulated rarefied generic and specialised knowledge and skills, which is enabled by and through the associatively constructed broad and deep culturally sensitive interpretive repertoire, these are Holt's HCCs. In contrast to these, LCCs are those who have experienced relatively enclosed and situated lives within tightly bound geographic and social communities. They, and their parents before them, have at most a secondary or vocational education and typically are, or were, employed in blue collar or low skill routinised white collar jobs. In many cases, material resources for these people are constrained, and managing the implications of this, is an immediate concern and focus. Consequently, the cultural knowledge, skills and inter-pretive horizons, of LCCs are tied to this realm of experience and socio-historic context. That is, relative to HCCs, the cultural capital of LCCs can be classified as limited in scope and scale.

Important to Holt's (1998) findings are that significant qualita-tive differences between the approaches to consumption and expe-riences of these two distinct categories of consumers exist. HCCs on the one hand are analytical in their consumption and deploy a range of evaluative frameworks and associated practices to extract individualised meanings and experiences form consumed products and activities. This, it is argued, is even the case with mass marketed goods and commodities. Although HCCs prefer, and selectively seek out authentic products and experiences, where unavoidable, they will deploy strategies and practices of re-appro-priation, creativity or juxtaposition to cleanse commodities of their marketer implied meanings or associations, that is they personalise or customise them. For HCCs, this is arguably a significant and essential skill and practice, where increasingly it is difficult to identify an experience, object or activity that has slipped the grasp of the market or, that has not been ascribed with commercially sig-nificant meanings by marketers (Kozinets 2002a). What is more, the HCCs in this sample held cosmopolitan tastes, had a predisposi-tion towards aesthetic consumption through connoisseurship and were accustom to boundary transgression and experimentation. For instance Holt (1998) describes how an informant (Kathryn) practiced 'combinatorial inventiveness' (p.16) in food consumption

6

and meal preparation through drawing on these resources and dispositions:

> We... start with a cold soup like vichyssoise or gazpacho, my husband makes a spicy Jamaican chicken with rice, or maybe trout sauced with red wine base with Cointreau, and make a big salad with bitter greens, and a different desert such as a great big soufflé or something like that. We have wine with meals and my husband makes planter's punch.
>
> (Informant Kathryn in Holt 1998: 16)

Finally the HCCs in this research sought self-actualisation through their consumption and leisure experiences. In this sense much of what is consumed and experienced is a means to fulfilling a range of integrated projects. HCCs have a strong value and disposition to learn and develop through consumption. Seemingly, they would seek out and prioritise those experiences that enable this in abundance but would also be drawn to extracting the detail and nuance from apparently mundane and everyday experiences and products. They would seek to individuate them.

Taking the liberty of imposing Holt's typologies on our sectors for insight, we can outline the range of products and experiences that may engage them. In pursuing they would be drawn to authentic offerings or those that are not overtly commercialised. They would relish products and experiences that would encourage the deployment of skill and creativity and ones that would allow for personal development and intellectual and spiritual growth. In this respect HCCs would identify with being classified as travellers rather than tourists. Preferring to construct their own holiday itineraries and seek to encounter the new, novel, the different, and interesting. They would be drawn to immersive experiences that challenged and enlarged their horizons. These consumers would achieve the goal of locating the authentic through entering 'the "world" of a different social milieu, rather than gazing at it from outside' (Holt 1997: 113). These consumption styles and tastes would be carried into the other fields of consumption covered by this book.

The reference to Holt's informant Kathryn offers insight in to the ways in which food is consumed. Food is selected and valorised for its authenticity, sensory characteristics, experiential and aesthetic quality and its potential to (re)connect them to nature, other cultures, and faraway lands. Combined with travel, HCCs would seek out indigenous and local cuisine to extend their eclecticism and stock of knowledge. Likewise restaurants are chosen against similar criteria, there would be a preference for the artisanal and the casual, and such consumers would not apportion much value on status-orientated restaurants or celebrity chefs (Holt 1998). Such an approach may be seen integral to the creation of extraordinary by these groups, and when combined with an ascetic value, it is likely that food choices and consumption would reflect sensitivities to culture, nature and the environment. In lieu of this, it is possible that HCCs would: be ardent supporters of local agricultural projects; value and utilise farmers' markets and local producers; and relish growing and producing their own food. This however would be balanced against the thirst to experience the novel and authentic character of distant and exotic cuisine. Over determining object signification as much of what Holt has to say is that market meanings, or meanings embedded in objects are inconsequential to consumption. It is the practices and experiences that offer the value to the HCC consumer. For example, being able to interact with the producers and their produce at the farmers' market and take in the multisensory and experience the gastronomic pleasures of their wares. The contemporary consumer acquires new skills and knowledge from consuming the cuisine of indigenous peoples of foreign climes.

LCCs on the other hand would be the tourists (the spectators, consumers, and the entertained). Holt (1997) reports that these consumers would be drawn to package deals and full service experiences. Disney World, cruises, beach and resort holidays and guided tours would feature heavily in their preferences and reflect their tastes. With food, given the concerns imposed by responding to the needs of everyday material reality, many LCCs would possibly be drawn to practical produce that is balanced within their financial means. Those of this strata who have achieved financial success and are not so constrained in this resource may favour premium packaged meals and branded products. This latter observation reflects Holt's (1997 and 1998) contention that 'the good life' for LCCs is understood against their background and lived experience of material scarcity. Previously denied the material pleasures of life, wealthy LCCs typically counterbalance this through consuming in abundance and valuing what is conventionally understood as luxury or scarce. This logic would extend to events and hospitality, where, material constraints would naturally impede and structure attendance and usage of such activities. Where this is the case, local activities would predominate, such as village fayres, community and family events such as weddings, children's parties, dinner parties, and school sports days, or be restricted to weekends and special occasions, such as birthdays, anniversaries, and religious events and rituals. Restaurant preference would be familiar wholesome cuisine where the dining experience is relatively informal and unconstrained. Buffet style concepts and practices that are characterised by autonomy and 'plenty' are typical examples of this (Holt 1998: 11). With unconstrained financial resources, tastes would be drawn to those activities and experiences that would demonstrate material abundance, luxury and entertainment. The latter value being mobilised by attempts to escape and balance the mundane reality of their everyday experience in routine and repetitive jobs. Possibly then, horse racing, attendance at major sporting events, becoming a season ticket holder of a supported football team, visiting the Clothes Show Live, or attending music events and gigs would now feature as exemplar activities. In a similar way, hospitality consumption would be upgraded to more frequent visits to restaurants, gastro pubs, and hotels that are marked out by some criteria or other, as those that are considered exemplary in their class. By criteria, we refer here to Michelin and AA stars, celebrity chefs, endorsement by restaurant critics, and consensus market views of a products superiority or status. However, it is important that we recognise the significance of consumption practices and their relationship to individual and group identities.

■ Consumption as identity

As stated previously, the things and experiences we buy, drive, wear, drink, eat, visit, the holidays we take, the restaurants we use or the events we attend all, become social makers of the type of person we are or more importantly the type of person we want to be seen as. For Holt (1998: 4) '...consumption is a particular status game that must be analyzed in isolation rather than lumped together with work, religion, education and politics...'. The significance of this for the individual is identified by Cova and Cova who argue that:

> ...we have now entered the era of the ordinary individual, that is to say an age in which any individual can – and must – take personal action, so as to produce and show one's own existence, one's own difference.
>
> (2002: 596)

As such, consumption becomes a source of identity (Miles 1996) and that on a daily basis we negotiate the symbols of consumer culture choosing which elements we engage with and in. The things we consume become a means of forming our identity, thus the choice to purchase a designer suit or dress often has nothing to do with the quality of the item, but has more to do with the message it sends to our peers about our knowledge of fashion, our ambitions and our taste, it becomes a badge or code of who we are, and is read by other consumers who then make assumptions about who we are. Thus, consumption is essentially a social activity that incorporates meanings within the culture in which we live. Consumers skilfully use goods to '...communicate, mark and classify social relations, it is a way of communicating individual taste, status, aspiration and even protest' (Izberk-Bilgin 2010: 307). This

6

reinforces Holt's view '...that the pursuit of individuality through consumption is a central characteristic of advanced capitalist societies' (1998: 13). What is important to re-state here is that although at first sight the relationship between consumption and identity can be seen as superficial it provides the freedom to create and shape an identity we want rather than having one imposed upon us by society. As Miles states:

> ...the evidence suggests that consumption performs the role of *solidifying* an individual's identity. In the context of cultural ramifications of peer relations amongst you people [*sic*], identities in a so called 'postmodern' world might well be argued to be far more stable than many commentators would be prepared to admit.
>
> (1996: 150)

The role of leisure, food, tourism and events is especially significant in the formation of identity as the activities are often very public, attending a cultural event makes a very public statement about your cultural knowledge, desires and aspirations. Additionally we often communicate our experiences and preferences by showing our holiday photographs, using social media and blogs such as Twitter, Facebook or TripAdvisor to express our views about restaurants and hotels etc. All of these activities provide us with the opportunity to advertise our levels of cultural capital and thus become expressions of identity.

■ Conclusion

This chapter has identified the significance of consumption in both the construction of our identity and cementing our position within particular groups, tribes or habitus. The consumption process has become one of the central elements in the formation of our identities and we are in a continual process of interaction with other consumers, whereby we exchange cultural capital with each other. Products and experiences that make us feel good are often rich in cultural capital, it becomes a significant element of the communication process. Tourism, events, hospitality and food are important aspects in our lives and are one of the major means by which we express our identities, preferences, taste and social or cultural standing. Experiences marketing utilises the elevated significance of these activities to create a world within marketing literature that reinforces the cultural significance of the activities, it uses a language, theme and symbolism that is appropriate to differing tribes or habitus'. This is a significant demarcation from traditional approaches to segmentation and communication as it privileges cultural and social movements over often quantitative oriented demographic approaches. It is also important to remind ourselves that marketing is all about people (their needs, desires, wants etc.) and communication, understanding our relationship to consumption places the individual, the person back in the centre of the process. Additionally, by understanding how cultural intermediaries generate trends and consumer desires it becomes possible to predict what is going to be the next big food, destination, hotel style or festival, which provides the marketer with a competitive advantage. Therefore, the next time one of your friends or colleagues is talking you through their holiday and showing you photographs, or are telling you about this great little restaurant they have found, think about how they are transmitting their cultural capital and think about what group, tribe or habitus they are aligning themselves with.

Interpreting Marketing

■ Introduction

There are certain assumptions within contemporary marketing about the consumer's behaviour, how they make decisions and how they understand marketing communications. As a result, marketers identify groups that are clustered together in neat market segments ranging from the macro level in which we target cultures or genders, to the micro where we target small groups of consumers that share similar backgrounds, income, education or locality etc. This approach assumes that these groups of consumers share a view of the world, a set of values and a level of knowledge that leads to a shared understanding and relationship to the product being promoted and the process of marketing. Although segmentations remains the dominant means of grouping consumers together and identifying target markets, this chapter relocates the individual consumer at the centre of the marketing process by recognising that each individual consumer or customer will bring with them their own experience, knowledge etc. That is, they are reflexive subjects who do not simply accept the messages propagated by marketers, but interpret, resist, negotiate and form their own perception of the marketing message. In order to gain and insight into how people understand marketing it is important to identify some of theoretical debates that go some of the way to explaining how individual's interpret the debates and discourses that underpin THEF marketing. Additionally, in order to understand the consumer's relationship to marketing communications it is important to understand how authors, organisations or professional bodies select and produce marketing texts, as the nature of the publication will also guide the final interpretation. For example the authors of this book come from differing academic traditions, one from a social science background and the other from a business tradition, however the content and structure of this book is guided by certain shared beliefs about the role of marketing in contemporary society and a dissatisfaction with the ways in which traditional marketing texts locate the consumer and the marketing process. Therefore this book reflects the knowledge base, the values and the reality of the two authors as white, middle-class university lecturers.

Just like the authors, each individual consumer or customer brings with them a set of knowledge, a view of their position in the world and their personal values. These are formed by their social and cultural backgrounds, their gender, their educational background, and their geographical location, the influence of their friends or families amongst other influences. These personal influences can be categorised as three distinct areas, epistemological, ontological and axiological (for good discussion of these aspects see Bryman 2004: 21–24). It is these areas of the individual's experience or personality that define the way in which they relate to the marketing process and the product or service being sold. These three areas can be simply defined as shown in Figure 7.1.

Epistemology (Knowledge base)	Ontology (Position in world)	Axiology (Value systems)
Relationship with marketing informed by	Relationship with marketing informed by	Relationship with marketing informed by
Knowledge How materials produced Authority of materials Individual's perception Individual's memory Individual's consciousness Individual's reason	Individual reality Individual influences Social and cultural background Class Education Religion Race Geographical roots	Their values Morals Informed by epistemology and ontology

Figure 7.1: Marketing and Epistemology, Ontology and Axiology

The implication for this is that every individual consumer, producer and marketer will come to the table with a differing set of knowledges, everyday lived experience/existence and set of values. Therefore we have to recognise that there are multiple worldviews or multiple realities. This has huge implications for the future of marketing as technological advances and the fragmentation of communication channels means that we can be more sophisticated in understanding how the consumer relates to the marketing process and ultimately how we engage and tailor approaches and communication channels for the multiple realities of segmentation.

■ The epistemology and ontology of marketing

Before we can understand how consumers interpret the marketing process, it is important that as a researcher or student you question how your own ontological and epistemological understanding of marketing has been formed, as ultimately this will direct the way in which you read and understand this book, and how you judge the contribution it makes to the field of marketing. Burrell and Morgan define epistemology as:

> Assumptions about the grounds of knowledge – about how one might begin to understand the world and communicate this as knowledge to fellow human beings.
>
> (1979: 4)

While Klein *et al.* define epistemology as:

> The nature of human knowledge and understanding that can possibly be acquired through different types of research and the appropriateness of the methods of investigation.
>
> (1991: 5)

In comparison, ontology represents a particular view of reality held by the consumer or individual. There are two main ontological possibilities that are useful in understanding how the consumer interprets THEF marketing. The first is that there is one reality and it is observable by a consumer who has little if any impact on the object being observed. The second is that reality consists of an individual's mental constructions of the objects with which they engage, and that the engagement impacts on the observer and the situation being observed (Titscher *et al.* 2000: 14; Guba and Lincoln 1989: 23). In summary, the analysis of the interpretation process needs to be frames within the consumer's knowledge and view of the world.

Phillimore and Goodson (2004) in undertaking a survey of tourism research have recognised five distinct epistemological and ontological 'movements'.

- **The first movement** is defined as the traditional period of tourism research, and is guided by a positivistic approach to tourism studies which are based upon '…predetermined rigid research agendas, studies that seek to quantify qualitative data, studies aimed at generating tourism typologies and studies that place little or no emphasis on methodological issues' (2004: 10–12).

- **The second movement** they define as the 'modernist approach' in which there is 'evidence of a shift to post-positivist modes of thinking, although with clear evidence that researchers continue to be convinced of the fundamental importance of maintaining positivist rigour' (2004: 15).

- **The third movement** is defined as 'blurred genres', they further state that; 'The Blurred Genre stage makes a distinct difference from the 'modernist' and 'traditional' phases as researchers begin to move away from natural science and recognise multiple approaches embracing a more creative, artistic approach to research' (2004: 14).

- **The fourth movement** they define as 'crisis in representation', which has led to a 'profound rupture in thinking' and is reflected in the importance that: '…the personal biography

7

of the researcher was critical in determining the way they approached research, and thus it was not possible, as had previously been argued, to simply replace one researcher with another and expect the same results, provided that the methods employed were unchanged. Instead of seeing research as a bigger process, researchers began to view all stages in the research as indistinct and overlapping. They acknowledged that there are multiple interpretations mediated by the personal biographies of researchers and their research subjects' (2004: 15–16).

- ■ **The final stage** which they define as the 'fifth movement' and which may be seen to have emerged from the fmourth movement as a result of the: 'Rapid social change and development of new social contexts make traditional approaches to research – those based on the notion that data can be interpreted objectively and then generalised to become a fact which reveals some knowledge about a singular reality – redundant'. (2004: 17).

However, the positivistic tradition continues to be the major influence in the construction of methodologies and THEF research (Botterill 2001; Phillimore and Goodson 2004). Delanty (1997) forwards five facets of positivism (scientism, naturalism, empiricism, value freedom and instrumental knowledge). In 'The epistemology of a set of tourism studies', Botterill (2001) examines these facets in relation to seven PhD projects each utilising a positivistic approach within a multidisciplinary study. His findings were that the adoption of a 'scientism' approach (in which the student used a social science and a physical science based methodology) led to:

Problematizing the interaction of people and nature in a tourism setting and preconditions the necessity of a merging of social and physical science epistemologies.

(2001: 203)

The claim to value freedom by all the students was disputed, as all applied 'a rich stock of subjective experience' (2001: 205) to their studies. The correlation between positivism and the production of 'technically useful knowledge' conventionally justified the approach. However, the expectation of producing useful knowledge meant that the research and the methodology were influenced by policy maker's perceptions and local state interventions. Therefore, for Botterill the adoption of a positivistic approach is fundamentally flawed.

The use of critical theory is almost completely absent from the study of THEF (Botterill 2001: 207; Phillimore and Goodson 2004: 15–16). The reason for this according to Botterill is that much tourism research focuses on a dominant industry agenda and is witnessed in the traditional approach to marketing.

The best way to achieve this is by recognising the movements and approaches that construct the academic subject of marketing. The complexity of marketing as a process, as a multidisciplinary cultural activity, as a form of communication or as the manifestation of power relations has formed a largely unrecognised and certainly unspoken ontological and epistemological tradition. The majority of marketing texts and journals are located within the fields of business management or applied marketing; this has created a significant body of empirically orientated data that has been underpinned by the positivistic tradition. Yet it is possible to question the viability of positivism as an appropriate and encompassing form of epistemology and ontology, as it may be seen to limit the ability of the researcher to adequately investigate the social and cultural world in which marketing is located.

■ The interactive consumer

An interesting way of conceptualising the contemporary consumer is to think of the consumer not as a passive participant within the marketing process, but to define them as an 'interactive participant' (see Kress and Van Leeuwen 2001). This allows us to think of marketing as an interactive dynamic cultural activity, in which all the stakeholders or participants in the process, from the commissioning company, to the marketers, students or consumer all engage in dynamic cultural interaction. It is within this interaction/mediation that the consumers draw from their epistemological, ontological and personal biographies (Guba and Lincoln 1989) to interpret, or negotiate the meaning and purpose of the text whether it is in the form of a brochure, flyer, radio/television advertisement or website etc. As stated previously in this book, the marketing of THEF often involves the semiotic construction of a language that is embedded with social, cultural and individual meaning, and is underpinned by a ludic/hedonistic or celebratory discourse. By interacting with marketing communications the consumer forms an emotional attachment to the experience by becoming an interactive participant in the marketing process. This interactivity relies on how the individual applies their epistemological (knowledges), ontological (being in the world) and axiological (values) foundations to the process. The impact of this reflexivity or interaction is to create multiple, individual and personal readings and interpretations.

Much human activity (including our relationship to experiences, products, and marketing texts), is devoted to ordering processes through the organisational patterning of experience by means of tacit, emotional meaning-making processes. We emotionally invest in products and services and marketing plays a significant role in this as it guides how we should interpret representations of THEF. Such a process identifies the consumer as an axis of experience and selfhood, in which we cannot be understood apart from our 'embeddedness' (Kress and Van Leeuwen 1996) in the social and symbolic systems of the culture or society in which we live. This 'embeddedness' is personally reinforced and expressed by our consumption patterns. For example, there are a number of recent television adverts that sell a lifestyle that is lived out through the consumption of tourism. In the case of the recent SAGA cruise commercials (2011) this locates the two lucky guests within a privileged formal environment of chauffeur-driven formally-dressed guests, all socialising within a particular elitist grouping. The consumption of such an experience demonstrates a view of the world and a set of individual values that become reinforced by consumption of joining the club. In the same way this also reflects residual cultural templates of deferred gratification, where you have earned the right during your working life to live out your twilight years in this pleasurable or hedonic environment. This aligns with the marketing segments known by the acronym SKIER (spending the kids' inheritance in early retirement) (Willetts 2011), in the same way this segment reflects an acknowledged high value resource with high accumulated assets and disposable income, for example recent estimated has placed a mean net asset value of £600,000 per household (Willets 2011).

Therefore the consumer then becomes central to the marketing/consumer dichotomy in which producers and consumers interact. However, in order to understand how the individual interprets experience marketing we need to understand how the symbolic authority of the text directs and influences the consumer's understanding and subsequent behaviour. As stated previously, the intangible nature of the tourism, hospitality, events and food product produced a reliance on the production of effective marketing materials that has become the recognised means of promoting the sector. As such, the consumer forms a particular relationship with the text in which it guides and signposts experience, adding to their personal biography and informing the consumer's 'being in the world' (Maloney 1993). Therefore there is an interrelationship between marketing materials and the individual consumer that leads to multiple interpretations even though the text may be generic for the producer.

7

■ Interpretation and marketing

All marketing materials whether in the form of a radio advertisement, product, logo or a simple flyer may be seen as vehicles for carrying the marketing message, transferring it from the marketer to the consumer. However, the nature of the sign vehicle, where it is physically placed in terms of form of communication (newspaper, radio station or pavement), context (time of year, reputation of communication or cultural understanding and significance of communication) and the individual's political, economic positioning or their social and cultural background will impact upon how the consumer reads and interprets the marketing communication. The impact of this on marketing practice is to inform our understanding of the elements that inform the consumer's interpretation of marketing texts. In order to develop an effective marketing strategy it is necessary to adopt a holistic and critical approach to marketing and this includes at the basic level understanding your customer.

As we will discuss in Chapter 8, the contemporary consumer is an amateur semiotician, as they negotiate the commercial world that surrounds everyday lived experience. It is argued that we negotiate somewhere in the region of 2000 advertisements every day. As we walk around we read the images and words that are contained within these advertisements, we interpret them, find meaning, reject them or get excited and change our behaviour or buy the product. As consumers we understand the language of contemporary marketing practice. This is particularly significant in the language of experiences marketing as it located in a particularly strong historical, social and cultural discourse (see Chapter 2) that surrounds THEF.

The reading and interpretation of marketing communications becomes a very personal and reflexive activity in which, as consumers we find our own meanings and understandings. Therefore, what we can say is that marketing communications signpost experience, they direct us, attempt to influence our perceptions and to ultimately inform our purchasing behaviour in favour of the product or experience we are marketing. The signposting of experience leads us on a journey in which we negotiate advertisements drawing from our depository of experiences and feelings that construct our worldview. The role of the marketer is to influence the way in which we negotiate these advertisements, to accept and privilege their message by following it in the marketing communication whether it be to change our eating habits, to escape on holiday or to celebrate through attending an event. Although the marketer can influence, signpost or guide interpretation it is important to recognise that the consumer is a free thinking reflexive individual who will draw on their experiences, values etc. to form an opinion and develop their own individual relationship to and with the product or experience. In order to understand the consumer's relationship to marketing communications we need to understand how the relationship is defined by the consumer's value systems.

■ The axiology of marketing: values

7

When we examine the axiology of marketing, we need to understand that brands, experiences and products will often be underpinned by a value system, what the product stands for, what it means to consumers. For example many food companies such as Cadbury's or Starbucks are adopting a 'Fairtrade' approach to their production of their products (see Chapter 9 for further information) whereby they are ensuring that their ingredients are ethically sourced. Many restaurants will advertise that their producers are locally sourced and organic, while destinations make claims about how sustainable their tourism product is. When organisations do this they are developing values that underpin the ethos of their company or add an ethical value to their brand. However, when examining how consumers relate to or interpret products and experiences, the consumer draws on their axiological foundations, or in other words, their value systems.

The consumer's interpretation can be seen as a cognitive or mental activity that locates the product within a value system and makes judgements as to how the product or experience fits into this. For example an 18–30 holiday brochure may be offensive to an older tourist with its representations of scantily-clad men and women, and the text which explores the more hedonistic tendencies of contemporary tourism. Each of us possesses a complex value system that we draw upon every time we attempt to interpret an advertisement. Our axiology or value system is developed from various experiences and knowledge we have collected over our lifetime from sources such as our social and cultural location/background, and is reflected in our inherent and learnt behaviour. Thus our value systems will vary according to where we live, our religion, ethnic background, school and education system, what books we have read, what television programmes we have seen, the values of our parents, friends and family and as such we will all make different value judgements as part of the interpretation and consumption process.

		Extrinsic	Intrinsic
Self Orientated	Active	**EFFICIENCY**	**PLAY**
	Reactive	**EXCELLENCE**	**AESTHETICS**
Other Orientated	Active	**STATUS**	**ETHICS**
	Reactive	**ESTEEM**	**SPIRITUALITY**

(Holbrook 1996, 1999)

Figure 7.2: Holbrook's Framework of Consumer Value

There are a number of value judgements we make during the consumption process and we need to understand how the consumer relates to our product or experiences. Holbrook (1996, 1999) presents a multidimensional framework (Figure 7.2) that offers a useful way of understanding the nature of consumer value. This framework is based upon a horizontal axis that denotes that value can be either *extrinsic*, in the sense that the consumption of a product or service is a means to another end, or *intrinsic*, which implies that something is consumed as an end in itself. The vertical axis then designates consumer value as both self or other orientated and active or reactive. *Self-orientated* value relates to those experiences that are pursued for the effects that they have on the consumer him or herself, and *other orientated* is where consumption is pursued either for, in the sake of, or the reactions and responses it gets from others. 'Others' being classified here as people and entities, such as the natural environment, faiths, religions, or realities such as different world orders and societies. Finally *active consumption* is that which requires 'the physical or mental manipulation' (Holbrook 1996: 3) of an object or activity to extract its value, and *reactive value* relates to the effects that an object or activity has on a consumer from their consumption of it.

As can be seen, Holbrook's framework aligns with the service and interaction logic of marketing which is defined in Chapter 3, as it is argued that value is relativistic and can only be realised or experienced through interacting with an object (consumer good) or engaging in an activity (service, deed, or performance).

■ Types of value

■ Efficiency

The nature of value here is located around the efficient use of consumer resources. As was discussed in Chapter 4, consumer resources take numerous forms. In this respect consumers who seek and create this form of value deploy marketplace objects that save money, time, space or cognitive effort. Examples include time-saving devices, products and processes such as online ticketing intermediaries like Ticketline or those used by budget airlines to streamline purchasing, as well as those targeted at grocery shoppers such as Tesco's bar code reader. In addition, convenience products such as ready meals and complementary products such as microwave ovens would also feature here. Quick-service restaurants and supporting infrastructure such as the drive-through or home delivery are other examples. Convenience is also positively correlated with location in some instances, and consumers may be drawn to utilising the facilities and products located nearest to them to save time. This correlation in many respects explains the development and rapid growth of convenience grocery formats such Sainsbury's Local, Tesco's Metro and M&S Food.

Efficiency can be expressed in financial terms, whereby budgeting would possibly be the main focus, and as result products and services would be selected that meet strict financial criteria. BOGOFs (buy one get one free) and other promotional offers by firms such as product or service bundling and discounts are marketing examples that relate to financial efficiency. Incentive schemes that are tied into loyalty packages offered by supermarkets, hotels and airlines could also be valuable to consumers from an efficiency perspective. Many of these allow numerous resources or benefits to be accumulated alongside purchases of products that feature within the loyalty scheme. For example Sainsbury's offers air miles with Easyjet in exchange for loyalty points that are accumulated alongside purchases through the Nectar card, while Hilton's loyalty scheme – Hilton Honors – offers incentives such as free overnight stays and deals on dining experiences. Consumers seeking efficiency may also be drawn to the products that feature within the budget segment of a market. For example, Formula 1 and Premier Inn within the hotel category, eat-all-you-can buffets or carveries may feature in the restaurant sector, and the basic, everyday value or essentials ranges of food retailers, out-of-season holidays and package deals, may also meet the efficiency criterion from a monetary perspective for some consumers. Finally, marketplace resources that save cognitive effort can be classified as those that reduce the amount of thought or length of the decision-making process. In this respect we could position all inclusive holiday packages, travel agents and tour operators who plan the inventory and provide the transportation for consumers of large-scale events such as music concerts, theatre performances or major sporting events within this debate. Marketing communications materials that are effectively targeted and produced may also fit here if they save a consumer having to expend effort in locating and evaluating them.

■ Excellence

Excellence relates to a product or services ability to provide a quality experience or perform its function in an excellent way. There is a huge literature on product and service quality (see Parasuraman *et al.* 1988; Buttle 1996; Lages and Fernades 2005; McCabe *et al.* 2007) which will not be reviewed here, but it is worth noting that quality is itself a multidimensional construct and is understood and evaluated by consumers in a variety of ways. For the sake of brevity we will simply state the quality is a subjective consumer judgement based upon an assessment of relative superiority or excellence across a single or combination of product feature/s, attributes, functionalities, performances, or a service or activity's ability to meet or exceed requirements. These judgements are made vis-à-vis the consumer's resources and effort that are invested in consuming the product or activity. These judgements could, for example in food, be based upon a product's taste relative to that of competitors, its price, or the expectations that have been set through the marketing effort or word of mouth recommendations, and a consumer's past experience with similar produce. In hospitality, a judgement could be made on relative service quality in terms of how attentive, empathic and responsive the service delivery personnel are. In events or visitor attractions, perceptions of excellence may be based upon an overall assessment of the servicescape (Bitner 1992) in respect of the physical and ambient characteristics of the venue in which the event takes place in combination with the actual delivery and performance of the event itself, and its communicative staging (Arnould *et al.* 1998; Chronis *et al.* 2012). It is worth noting that consumers' judgements and expectations will often be predicated on an organisation's market positioning, in the sense that excellence will be sought and expected from those organisations, products and brands that promise to deliver it. So for example where a company claims that 'This is not just food', or that their role and responsibility to consumers is 'To fly. To serve', or that they offer a 'Luxurious retreat for the busy traveller' alongside the promise 'To treat a stranger as one of your own' (these, in sequential order being a combination of positioning statements and strap-lines of Marks and Spencer Food, British Airways, and Shangri-la Hotels respectively), they offer a value proposition of excellence and accordingly will be selected and evaluated by consumers against this criterion.

■ Status

Holbrook (1999) broadly defines status-orientated consumption as the set of consumer behaviours where the end result and goal is to achieve favourable responses from others. We develop this concept further, alongside that of esteem (see below) in Chapter 6 where we re-frame it as cultural capital endowments and resources. Status through this lens is a purposeful attempt to achieve social distinction or to seek acceptance and membership within social groups though the acquisition, use, and appropriation of products, activities or services. In this sense it is a goal-directed consumer behaviour through which one seeks recognition and a position (often an elevated one) within a social group and hierarchy. So for example the socially visible purchase and use of scarce and high value items like a bottle of Domaine de la Romanee-Contis Romanee-Contri Grand Cru, or attendance of elitist sporting events like the Cartier Queens Cup or Royal Ascot may be directed at realising this value for those who seek elite financial status. That is to say this form of consumption is a demonstration of a consumer's material resources, economic mastery and one's position within the economic pecking order. In a similar way the demonstration of a consumers knowledge of real ales or micro brewery beers through public lectures or invited talks may be undertaken to build status within this particular field. Eating at the chef's table in a Michelin starred restaurant is another illustration of how this value may be realised, but this time within the field of fine dining. Accordingly status consumption can be operative in a range of distinct consumption fields and spaces, from allotments where people compete for recognition through growing their own food, through to expeditionary travel pursuits such as commercially organised climbing experiences to Mount Everest (Tumbat and Belk 2011).

■ Esteem

Holbrook (1996: 4) argues that esteem is 'the reactive counterpart to status'. It is similar in its reputational effects, but rather than actively pursuing these effects, they are merely experienced passively by or through consequence of ownership of a good or engagement in an activity or service. Although esteem is passive, it is important and valuable to consumers nonetheless. This is explained through the distinction that while status is about 'getting ahead' and standing out, esteem is often correlated with belonging, 'fitting in', or marking out what lifestyle/s or role/s one aligns with (Holbrook 1999). In this respect, while a specific consumer's motivation may not be focused on building esteem, because of the social nature of consumption it will always possibly have these effects. So while a backpacker may be pursuing an ulterior motive such as play or spiritual experience, they will be generating social capital that will mark them out as belonging to a specific lifestyle. This logic holds for the connoisseur of exotic or local foods who will, as a consequence of their consumption and tastes, be classified socially as a 'foodie'.

■ Play

For Holbrook (1996), play is about having fun and engaging in ludic activity. In this respect we can situate a broad range of consumer experiences and products from all of our sectors in this category.

For example, many food products draw upon the repertoire of play and fun in their market positioning. Pringle's snacks for instance, endorse the value of play through the strap-line 'once you pop you can't stop' and the imagery of sharing and parties used in their advertising and packaging. Many supermarkets also produce packaged 'finger' and 'bite-sized' foods that are designed with parties and celebrations in mind. Food itself is often the centrepiece to celebration and ritual such as weddings, birthdays and Christmas (see Belk 1993 for discussion of the commercialisation and de-sacralisation of this ritual). In travel and tourism we can situate hedonically positioned youth package holidays, such as Thomas Cook, Club 18–30. Ibiza and Faliraki are now well known as party islands, and Monaco and the region of the Côte d'Azur as the playground of the rich and famous. At the extreme, there are also concepts designed for the liberally minded adult consumer such as hedonism resorts. We can also classify certain tourist activities in the realm of play such as skiing, snowboarding or whitewater rafting. In hospitality and events we have an equally broad range of products and experiences that may fulfil this value, such as pop concerts, bars, nightclubs and informal and themed diners, such as Franky and Benny's or France's Buffalo Grill. To this end we can reflect upon contemporary expressions that relate to the experiences sought from interacting with these products, such as 'blowing off steam', or 'letting your hair down'. From this review it is clear to see that play is central to the experience of many products that are marketed and consumed within our sectors, and hedonism is a key element of the consumer experience.

■ Aesthetics

Aesthetic consumption is self-orientated and autotelic. In experiencing this value, a consumer will interact with a product for personal enjoyment and pleasure, and to extract its fine and idiosyncratic qualities. To this end, aesthetic consumption is appreciative, and is often, but not always, accompanied by connoisseurship.

Accordingly, a product is appreciated as an end in itself, and is evaluated through a range of aesthetic criteria that an individual consumer brings to bear in their interaction with it. It is common knowledge that wine can be consumed to appreciate its organoleptic qualities, and this is the case for many fine, authentic, and exotic foods and beverages. This logic holds for the consumption of classical music or artwork for many consumers, except that the assessment of organoleptic qualities are switched to assessments based upon auditory, visual and emotional criteria. Thus the motivation to attend a cultural event, such as the Royal Academy of Arts annual exhibition, or Glyndebourne Opera Festival may be based around the aesthetic experience and value. Likewise a consumer may immerse themselves into some wilderness, landscape or urban setting for the sake of experiencing its beauty, or to admire its features and qualities.

■ Ethics

Experiences that allow consumers to express moral duty or obligation can be classified as ethical ones. Here a consumer is drawn to, or repelled by, those products and services that align to a consumer's ethical criteria or which allow him or her to make a difference, or not, to some identifiable 'other'; such as a culture, population, production practice, economy, or environment. As such, individuals are consuming ethically and realising this value when they purchase fair trade products or organic food, or additionally, when they select those that use less intensive methods in their production such as free range eggs. Recycling or reusing packaging, oils and containers from leftover food, may also be entangled within an ethical consumer framework. For others the vegetarian or vegan lifestyle may be pursued through a sense of moral obligation or through a distaste of poor animal welfare standards or farming practices, or by the livestock industry per se. Companies that subscribe to strict environmental guidelines, policy or criteria, may be considered to be ethically responsible and rewarded by patronage

7

and advocacy as a result. Likewise those that seem to be sensitive to the wider socio-cultural and ecological environment and behaving accordingly in their marketing and business practices, may benefit form similar effects, that is, they may be rewarded by consumers who seek such value and egalitarian commitment and sentiment. Importantly those companies that do not may be vilified and treated accordingly through boycotts or consumer activism. Due to the apparent and amplifying importance of ethics and sustainable marketing practice we have dedicated a chapter to these issues, so will leave the review at this point and direct the interested reader to this content (Chapter 9).

■ Spirituality

Spirituality relates to the sacred and humanistic aspects of consumption. Holbrook (1999) places here those experiences that produce feelings of ecstasy or transcendence, are in themselves magical, or those which portray and demonstrates one's adoration, alignment or appreciation of faith. As such, we can easily classify and align certain foods, food practices, and religious rituals that have food at the centre, with the latter of these definitional constructs. Within the Hindu faith for example, food is literally a gift from god and is treated accordingly, with great respect. In the more commercial sphere we also have those foods that are related to religious events such as Easter eggs or Christmas cake. We also have foods related to religious practices such as the bread and wine of Holy Communion, or the fasting associated with Ramadan. Pilgrimage is an aspect of faith and spiritual experience that would also feature in accordance with our sectors, people from all faiths make great journeys that span the globe to pay respect and homage to their spiritual leaders and theological values. Likewise, both small and large-scale events are organised and attended for the purpose of worship and celebration of deities and belief systems. An example of this is the Jehovah's Witnesses Convention which is staged at the Ricoh Stadium, Coventry and is attended by 15,000 worshippers.

With regards to the former of Holbrook's aspects of spirituality, a review finds that the literature is full of examples of marketplace activities and consumer behaviours that produce magical and extraordinary experiences. These are often predicated on Belk *et al.*'s (1989) seminal and foundational paper on the sacred and profane in consumer behaviour. A central notion of this study is that spiritual experiences and the sacred are now as much located in the commercial world and experienced through consumption, as they are in the field of religion. Thus we have studies that catalogue, but are not limited to, how consumers:

1 Are rewarded with transcendental, transformative and magical experiences, while finding communion with nature through participating in guided white water rafting excursions (Arnould and Price 1993; Arnould *et al.* 1999; Price *et al.* 1995);

2 Find communitas and momentarily experience utopia through Star Trek conventions (Kozinets 2001) and anti-market events like the Burning Man Festival (Kozinets 2002a);

3 Extract peak experiences and ecstasy through raving and clubbing (Goulding *et al.* 2009) and the consumption of music and art (Panzarella 1980);

4 Experience combinations of these phenomena through embarking upon extraordinary journeys and engaging in frontier travel (Laing 2006).

Once again, because of the significance of the spiritual and sacred to consumption within our sector we cover these issues in more detail in Chapter 2.

It is only through interaction that value can be experienced, and in this respect it is implied that consumers are the ones who experience value subjectively and individually based upon:

1 Their expectations of the value that they wish to extract or experience from their interactions with a product, service or

activity. Of special note here is the fact that different consumers may approach the same product for different experiences and for different forms of value. For example one could consume a fine wine for status, or to appreciate its organoleptic qualities through connoisseurship. The same wine could also be opened and shared as part of a ritualistic experience and event such as celebrating Christmas or somebody's birthday.

2 Their past experiences and history with the same or similar products. Here the consumer may weigh up if a previous encounter or experience with a product or service met their expectations and provided the sought value. Equally they may consider the potential of repeating, replicating, or enhancing that experience through future use.

3 How they perceive this product relative to competitor offers or experiences.

4 What they make of an experience based upon a preference judgement that is based upon a combination of the proceeding three factors and the weight of resources that they invest in it.

Although our epistemological background or world view is central to the interpretation process, within the marketing context, values or axiology becomes one of the dominant themes and there is a continual movement by companies and organisations to add to, improve or reinforce the value statements/propositions of their organisations and through the communication of these values build a relationship with the consumer. Returning to the SAGA Cruise example, the commercial expresses the values of SAGA and attempts to match them with the identified market segment. They enter into a shared world of experience, expectations and values, as such they come to share the same worldview or epistemology. In this way marketing can be seen as a process that seeks to match and merge/or produce a view of the world that the consumer could conceivably locate themselves and find value.

■ Conclusion

We often take for granted that consumers will understand and interpret generated meanings contained within products, communications or brands. Although marketing can significantly influence the interpretation process, the consumer is still a free thinking reflexive individual who will use their world view and value system to find meaning. It is important that we recognise this as it is easy to treat a consumer as part of one large market segment or demographic grouping. Although we can guide interpretation we must recognise that every individual will find their own meaning, will negotiate and often resist the marketing of experiences etc. Often the adoption of an overly prescriptive communication will deter the consumer as it does not provide room for the individual to find their own meaning, and as a result they will not purchase the product. The marketing of THEF requires a careful signposting of experience that leads the consumer, but at the same time provides a space in which they can find individual meaning and significance and may express their epistemology, ontological and axiological preferences. The next chapter examines how the semiotic language of THEF is developed and meaning is signposted within contemporary marketing.

7

 # The Semiotics of Experience

■ Introduction

This chapter examines how signs and sign systems, are utilised in marketing to give meaning and award value(s) to tourism, hospitality, events and food (THEF) products, activities and experiences. It also seeks to portray the dominant semiotic codes and signifiers presently operative in each of these sectors. This chapter will draw to a close with a critical examination of the power effects of these representation systems and practices. The meaning production process, which has its roots in the structural linguistic science and philosophy of semiotics is recognised as an integral and fundamental constituent of marketing practice (e.g. McCracken 1986; Mick *et al.* 2004; Mick and Oswald 2006; Oswald 2012). It is integral to the marketing communication process, the meaning of products and brands, the design and configuration of servicescapes and retail environment and, market segmentation and positioning more generally. By examining the semiotic structure that constitutes the various forms of marketing practice, objects and materials that are located and utilised within our sectors, it is possible to identify a semiotic language, or code, that is used by marketers and frames marketing practice. These meanings are intended to be read and understood by the consumer and other marketplace stakeholders for the purpose of achieving numerous marketing goals and ends. What is more, it is also considered to be essential to the understanding of specific consumption practices within the THEF sectors and consumer behaviour generally. This is based upon the premise that consumers exist within a semiotic system of signs, they resultantly become integral nodes within this system and, are compelled into thinking and behaving symbolically. That is they symbolically interact in the world socially and experientially, they interact with symbolic products, engage in symbolic activities and engage in symbolic experiences.

■ Semiotics and the significance of signs

Semiotics is very simply the study of signs and systems of representation.

> Signs are *simply* anything that stands for something (its object/*referent*), to somebody (interpreter), in some respect (its context, *i.e. in an advert, label, package, servicescape or retail environment*).

> (Mick 1986: 198, emphasis added)

Therefore, as consumers or citizens we are all amateur semioticians. We are surrounded by signs from the moment we awaken in the morning until we go to bed at night, signs essentially make the world intelligible and meaningful to us, they tell us when we can cross the road, which door to use and how we can exit a building. In the main we all understand the meaning of these sorts of signs, this is possible because we read, interpret and comprehend them. Comprehension in this case is made possible from belonging to a shared cultural context and system of meaning that frames and directs our reading and understanding. In the literature this context is sometimes referred to as the code (e.g. Alexander 2000; McCracken and Roth 1989; Holt and Cameron 2010) or a cultural template (Thompson and Arsel 2004). Essentially these codes or templates provide an interpretive or organising framework through which signs make sense and, things in the world come to have personal and social significance. A good example of this is to think about a

8

set of traffic lights, we all recognise and understand the function they perform: through historical convention and experience we equate the colour red with danger so we stop; green connotes safety so when the green light shows we know to proceed. Therefore, these rule based systems or organising frameworks allows us to make sense of everyday reality and navigate our experience in the world. Codes also allow us to read into someone's communicative intentions even when drawing upon the most arbitrary of signs. For example it is only through experience and being privy to the code that: the cowboy comes to symbolise rugged individualism (Solomon 2013; McCracken 1993), the cafetière becomes a representation of the self-proclaimed British middle classes (*Britain Thinks* 2011); and Hugh Fearnley-Whittingstall turns into a totemic symbol of the Bourgeoisie-Bohemian (Bo-Bo) contemporary ascetic lifestyle (Holt and Cameron 2010). With regards to the latter, on top of Holt and Cameron's insightful treatise, the interested reader should turn to McCracken (1989) for a discussion of the semiotics of celebrities and the cultural foundations of the endorsement process.

As codes are accumulated and assimilated through our lived experience and interactions with material and social reality in everyday life, they are not always and already universally shared. That is to say, they may vary between individual consumers and particularly across different market segments, such as age cohorts, ethnic groups or lifestyle sub cultures. In this respect where we are unfamiliar with the rules or do not understand the code in use, we may experience discomfort, disorientation, or surprise, and struggle to interpret and make sense of what confronts us. For example while it is no surprise to find coffee being sold in branded paper cups or oversize mugs from specialised dedicated retailers in the UK, we may be uncertain of the product if confronted by coffee being served over ice in plastic bag but research by Denny and Sunderland (2002) and Sunderland and Denny (2007) found that this is the dominant mode of consuming this commodity in

Bangkok. Equally this research also found that coffee in Bangkok has no 'clearly' identifiable place, unlike familiar elsewheres, coffee is not found in cafes, or specialised shops, it is sold instead by street vendors from market stalls. In sum, the cultural template or code, and the semiotic chain of symbols and signs that mark it out, and in which direct the production and consumption of coffee in this part of Thailand is very different to the one that frames and signposts these value creating activities in Europe and the USA and other parts of the world such as the rapidly developing metropolitan regions of China and Brazil.

■ The nature of signs

In our meaning-laden world pretty much anything and everything can be treated as a sign and, can be seen to hold semiotic potency and value. In fact nothing in the world is semiotically redundant; even nothing itself. In this way the world and its components, can be treated as text or narrative, just like a novel, things in, and of the world, are read for meaning, they have discursive significance. Clothing for example has textual properties, and is often read in this way (McCracken and Roth 1989). Arguably it is the semiotic of fashion that awards it its value and it is the meanings encoded in certain styles of attire and dress that visually mark out a Hipster from either a Goth or Psycho-billy or a colleague at Tesco from a customer. With experiences marketing then, the dress of service personnel must therefore be recognised as carrying symbolic significance and managed accordingly.

More so, THEF products and activities themselves carry and communicate meaning (Levy 1959) as do the practices and styles of consumption deployed by consumers in their efforts to extract value and meaning from using and interacting with them (Holt 1998). Kniazeva and Venkatesh (2007) for example have examined the meanings carried by specific food products and related consumption practices in the USA. Their findings portray a plethora

8

of competing meanings and associations, these include amongst other things, romance, bonding, friend, enemy, guilt, shame, solace, comfort, power, harmony, fun, love and hate. There are also products, activities and experiences that, because of their sign value and the way in which they are consumed, mark out time and impose a temporal social order on the world (Moisander and Valtonen 2006). Products like quiche, ice-cream, Pimms, and strawberries and cream, and co-production practices like growing your own food, mark out the boundaries between the seasons for example. While:

> people have a cup of coffee... when they take a break from work... or have a bottle of beer after work to create an end for the work day and to liberate themselves from work-related matters.
>
> (ibid: 11)

It is argued that these latter types of products, when set within and consumed in these experiential contexts, 'come to embody and reproduce the Western myth of freedom' (ibid: 11). In line with this argument it is possible that many of the products that constitute the THEF sectors may act in this way, when consumed to produce or mark out free time and leisurely activity. Thus it can be argued that the meaning and significance of products and experiences semiotically structure reality and our experiences of, and in, the world. We will return to these ideas later in the chapter were we describe the specific semiotic codes and language utilised in our sectors.

Interpersonal interactions also have symbolic significance (see Solomon 1983 for review). People search for meaning and understanding, both through verbal and non-verbal communication. We are all familiar with the lay phrase that 'actions speak louder than words', well this is true in semiotic terms, as all actions have sign value. In the same way so do expressions, utterances, and the use, display or otherwise appropriation of material objects, activities, and artefacts. Therefore, service personnel involved in the staging of THEF experiences must be mindful of the meanings they are transferring through their actions and interactions, as must those who are responsible for managing their behaviour and performance.

■ The order of signs

Much of what is discussed above is reminiscent of Saussarian semiotics (Saussure 1983) but, from the pioneering work of Pierce (1974), it is now generally accepted that signs can be classified into a taxonomy of three general categories, these are, in no particular order icons, indexes, and symbols. What marks these categories out from each other is the difference in the relationship between the sign (signifier) and its object (the signified).

First is the *icon,* this is a sign that imitates or has a resemblance or close correspondence to its object. Drawing on the multi-sensory nature and characteristic of our sectors, an iconic signifier could therefore look, sound, smell, taste, or feel like that which it signifies. Accordingly, iconic signs that may be found in THEF marketing materials or contexts could include amongst others: the sound of gun shots or explosions in battlefield recreations; the smell of the everyday lived experience of our ancestors at the Jorvik Viking Centre in York, or the spritzed essence of the seashore that may accompany your fish supper at Heston Blumenthal's restaurant, the Fat Duck. They could also be; a cartoon representation of a patriarchal Italian family in a pasta sauce advert; a performer adorned in a Roman centurion uniform or staged as a male mine worker at an heritage centre or within an advertisement for a living museum; or the plastic lemon shaped packaging that contains Jif lemon juice.

In this respect iconic signs permeate THEF experiences. They are integral to both the substantive and communicative staging of servicescapes and retail environments as well as being constitutive elements and component parts of advertisements, promotional materials, websites, and food packaging. With regard to the terminology used above 'substantive staging refers to the physical

8

creation of contrived environments', that is, their material configuration, while communicative staging includes the scripts, role performances and interactions that signpost and pattern consumer experiences in servicescape environments (Arnould *et al.* 1998: 90). For example, the use of French speaking waiting staff, stylised menus, music and décor that draws upon themes of Frenchness, a consumer can be momentarily transported semiotically to a provincial context and setting (Arnould *et al.* 1998). Alternatively, another consumer may perceive this to be a crass attempt at mimicry of an already artificial (inauthentic) representation of reality.

Secondly, the relationship between an object and an *indexical* sign is marked out by a causal relationship. Ecthner (1999) for example explains that a suntan is an index of sun exposure, while in a similar way, drunkenness is an index of excessive drinking and, Louis Roederer Crystal Champagne is an index of the nouveaux riche and celebrity party culture. The latter, of course, requires knowledge of the cultural code that awards this particular indexical relationship with its meaning, and by the same token this underlies why a suntan in some instances can also be an index of rugged individualism or healthiness (ibid).

Thirdly, a *symbol* is a sign that has an arbitrary association to its object which works through processes of social and cultural convention. For example, one of the dominant semiotic conventions utilised within tourism brochures is the use of the deserted beach. This image not only visually approximates – the 'materiality' of the destination we may be visiting, that is, its *denotative* meaning, it also signifies various potential consumer experiences. These can range from, amongst others, notions of escape, luxury, authenticity, fun, or romance. In this way the deserted beach signifies something to each individual consumer, it is not just a beach, but in a way it defines the experience of holidaying and being a tourist, it creates desire and expectation. The image of the beach comes to hold individualised *connotative* associations and significance. These meanings are dynamic and may change over time or in different situations and contexts based upon changes in a consumer's expectations, goals or projects, or modifications to their socio-cultural milieu and surroundings, or indeed the code presently operative.

■ Semiotics and the polysemic nature of objects and experiences

The latter statement of the preceding paragraph essentially implies that an object can be represented by many signifiers, in this way an object can stand for, or mean literally anything, this is down to processes involved in both production and consumption of signs, this in itself allows for the polysemic nature of consumption, experiences and meanings. Here lies both the power and peril of marketing, the signifier can be decoupled from its referent, it is possible for a marketer to imbue their products, activities and experiences (social objects) with multiple meanings. Accordingly a social object can be simultaneously positioned towards different markets or segments by using different signifiers and associations. Likewise the meaning of a social object can be adapted, tweaked or changed in accordance with marketplace trends or demands. Here lies the rub however, in the same way that marketers can switch and mix the symbolic significance of their social objects, so can consumers or others who have an interest in the meaning or significance of an organisation's products or practices (or in the values, espoused or otherwise, of the organisation itself).

An evaluation of Adbuster campaigns for example, illustrates how marketplace activists are taking on marketers and corporations at their own game by using established marketing methods and techniques. Through imitating their practices these groups are challenging the sign value and meanings of companies like McDonald's by producing adverts with countervailing and oppositional meanings and associations. One particular example of a print advert targeted against McDonald's uses an image of a person lying

8

on an operating bed who is connected to an electrocardiography (ECG) machine and surrounded by medical practitioners performing surgery. The pattern reported on the screen of the ECG looks as if it is within a normal range until it spikes to form two large arcs. These arcs bear a striking resembles to the golden arches logo of McDonald's. Text below carries the message 'Big Mac attack'. The pattern on the ECG machine then moves to a flat line suggesting that the patient has moved into cardiac arrest.

■ Semiosis and meaning transfer

This chapter outlines a general theory for marketing that suggests that marketers use signs and sign systems to encourage and (re) produce marketplace behaviours and experiences by loading products and experiences with meaning and significance. This process which is labelled semiosis (Bains 2006) or meaning transfer (McCracken 1986) is critical to contemporary marketing practice and marketing success, as we inhabit a world in which consumers are said to purchase meanings rather than functional benefits (Levy 1959) or utilise market-based resources to create their own meaning laden identities and lifestyles (Arnould and Thompson 2005). This is not to mention how significant the marketplace and the consumption of goods and experiences are in structuring reality and imposing an order to, and around the lives of individual consumers, and consumption collectives, as described above, and in Chapter 6.

Furthermore, the significance of marketing as a practice of semiosis is heightened with THEF experiences as the majority of customers have to be persuaded to purchase an experience before seeing it, and then if persuaded, will move into engaging in protracted consumption episodes and performances that may span several minutes, hours or weeks. In the case of the former, adverts, websites and brochures will be employed and used to communicate information and meaning but also to build anticipation, and showcase experiences. For example, due to the problem of intangibility, we will be shown images of a festival that may have been gathered the previous year, and this will seek to mitigate the risk of purchase and build anticipation by promising that type of experience. Secondly, these experiences often but not always unfold within the servicescape or managed context of the host organisation, and customers will need signposts to direct and narrate their experience. In these cases both the substantive and communicative staging are central to this process and should be managed not only for value but also for meaning and significance.

As marketers it is essential that we understand this semiotic language, and semiotics more generally. In order to convey specific meanings to marketplace stakeholders, and award significance to THEF experiences, we must be able to competently identify and select suitable (units of meaning or) signs (and arrange them in meaningful and compelling ways) through understanding the range of semiotic conventions and cultural codes which support them and award them their significance. What is more we also must become adept at reading culture and accounting for changes in the semiotic codes and conventions that award signs their potency and relevance. That is to say we must strive to be conversant with, and cogent of, the residual, dominant, and emergent cultural codes that animate and structure the market for experiences and award them their value (Alexander 2000).

■ The semiotics of tourism and events

The semiotics of tourism and events is not a new subject area; it has been developed and discussed by a number of authors who have identified its significance (Uzzell 1984; Culler 1988; Dann 1996a; Hopkins 1998; Echtner 1999; Jenkins 2003; Berger 2007; Thurlow and Aiello 2007), while MacCannell (1999: 3) goes as far as to state that 'there is a privileged relationship between tourism and semiotics'. Critically however, although a clear connection exists between tourism, events and semiotics, it has not been developed as a distinct movement in marketing literature even though it underpins the promotion process. Further, it is surprising that the area has not been developed to any great extent when you consider that Crick (1989) defined 'the semiology of tourism' as being one of the three main strands of tourism research. This view is supported by Dann who states:

> nowhere...is a semiotics perspective considered more appropriate than in the analysis of tourism advertising with its culture coded covert connotations, in the study of tourism imagery and in treatment of tourism communication as a discourse of myth.
>
> (1996a: 61)

For Culler 'Tourism is a practice of considerable cultural and economic importance' (1988: 153) and as such, tourism becomes an, 'exemplary case for the perception of sign relations' within contemporary society (Culler 1988: 162). Thus for Culler, the relationship between semiotics and tourism both 'advances the study of tourism' and '...in turn enriches semiotics in its demonstration that salient features of the social and cultural world are articulated in the quest for experience of signs'(ibid.: 165). Yet despite the recognition of the importance of semiotics within tourism and events management studies, little theoretical development has taken place in terms of developing semiotics from the purely abstract.

The application of semiotics within tourism and events has been theoretically applied as a label for the signs, images, and representations and to a certain degree the experiences of the consumer. For example, Urry states that:

> One learns that a thatched cottage with roses around the door represents 'ye olde England', or the waves crashing on to rocks signifies 'wild, untamed nature'; or especially, that a person with a camera draped around his/her neck is clearly a tourist.
>
> (2001: 139)

Or similarly, as Culler comments:

> All over the world the unsung armies of semioticians, the tourists, are fanning out in search of the signs of Frenchness, typical Italian behaviour, exemplary Oriental scenes...
>
> (1988: 158)

Such statements assume that all consumers are 'amateur semioticians' (Urry 2001), all interpreting and reading the signs and images presented by the industry within the same manner and, searching for the same types of experiences . Although both Culler and Urry refer to the consumer as semioticians, the designation of visitors as semioticians is questionable as there is a difference between reading signs in practice and being a semiotician. Yet even though the signs and images utilised by the experience industry 'signpost' experience (Jenkins 2003), the individual interpretation/reading of these signs and images is an individual activity in which we draw from our own backgrounds and experiences adding a complexity to the perceived relationship between tourism, events and semiotics.

It is easy to oversimplify the relationship between semiotics and events or tourism, as there is a lack of clarity within the definition of semiotics in terms of phraseology, method and definition of what a sign stands for. Smith (2005) has undertaken a substantial semiotic analysis of Barcelona which has gone some of the way to clarifying terms within tourism studies by examining how that city has been represented in the tourism literature and what these representations mean to tourists prior to them visiting the destination. Additionally, Jenkins (2003) in her analysis of the relationship between photographs within travel brochures and backpackers' experiences of destinations in Australia examined how the signs and images backpackers saw before they went to the destination impacted upon where they visited and what photographs they took while there. This research found that where there was a strong or dominant image that was used in tourism marketing such as Sidney Harbour Bridge or the Eiffel Tower in Paris, then tourists

8

were drawn to them and they would have their photograph taken in front of it to mark that they had been there, and the photograph itself would them become a semiotic marker of this excursion. Similarly Hopkins (1998) examined the frequency of certain signs and images within a number of tourism brochures for the Lake Huron region of Canada. His findings were that marketing focused on certain myths or significant tourism attractions such as the Tower of London, the Empire State Building or the Taj Mahal and these are elevated to almost a mythical status, but once we go there we are often disappointed as they do not live up to the images we have seen in brochures or on television. Hopkins explains this in the following way; 'Imagination and desire fuel place-myths, but familiarity and dashed expectations will dissolve them' (1998: 66). The significance of this is that we give places a semiotic meaning within tourism and events, people accept these meanings and it informs their decision to visit and place, and also what experience they should get when they get there.

■ The semioticlanguage of tourism

As the interpretation process involves a certain degree of emotional involvement, we need to understand how the semiotics of tourism and events builds this relationship with the consumer. There are a number of conventions that underpin definitions of contemporary tourism and events and include certain themes and signs that construct the experience of expected. The first element of the language of tourism and events marketing involves the semiotic construction of a time and place in which the experience is located. Often the marketing text offers the consumer entry into a time and space that is removed from everyday lived experience or can be perceived as 'extraordinary' (Urry 2001). This is demonstrated in the use of phraseology in tourism and events marketing that focuses on the use of emotive words and images that offer 'once in a lifetime experience' or 'escape', 'luxury', 'unspoilt', 'exciting' etc. By analysing tourism, events, hospitality and food marketing texts, it is possible to identify themes of words and images that construct the language of experience. Figures 8.1, 8.2 and 8.3 identify the text and image themes that underpin contemporary marketing practices, there are certain themes that run through all categories, and often revolve around, escape, authenticity and time/space.

Language of tourism Semiotic themes	Language of events Semiotic themes
Escape Luxury Exciting Freedom Different notions of time and space Experience Friendly Untouched Authentic Play	Extraordinary A carnival Unique Once in a lifetime Festival Celebration Fun Exciting Authentic Cannot miss

Figure 8.1: Semiotic themes

■ The Semiotics of food and hospitality

The semiotic representations of hospitality and food are socially and culturally embedded within contemporary marketing practices. This embedding forms a marketing language of hospitality and food that draws from a long historical discourse that locates food and hospitality at the centre of nearly all cultures (O'Connor 2005; O'Gorman 2007; Claseen 2007). Although the concept of hospitality and food is a significant element of culture, its marketing needs to be contextualised within the time in which it is being judged and as such reflects trends in food, diet, cuisine, health. For example the use of images and themes taken from the slow food movement and more organic forms of production within food marketing campaigns provides a refuge from fast food culture and the instantaneous nature of postmodern society (Delind 2006), even if they are being used to promote fast food restaurants or ready meals. The semiotic representations of food and hospitality often elevates the experience by offering links to pleasure, fun and sophistication. Fantasia (1995) defines these as 'pleasure zones'. Food and hospitality marketing creates a utopian space in which the experience or expectation of experience is elevated to a rarefied level beyond the everyday lived experience of eating food as merely food. The representation of food or restaurants in adverts, on menus or packaging as organic, authentic, luxurious or space semiotically signifies a 'graceful way of living' (Delind 2006: 128), it bounds our past and memory creating a sense of belonging by drawing on the embedded definitions of hospitality and gastronomy.

The semiotic consumption of hospitality and food by the consumer within advertising is an 'authoritative act' that 'authenticates' (Marshall 2005: 73) our identity and position within the world as it acts as a social marker of who we are (Gvion and Trosler 2008). The campaign draws us into the semiotic consumption process, the represented dining experience, the available food choices, the type of drink we are attracted to act as 'agency of culinary culture, lifestyle and systems' (Gvion and Trosler 2008). For example, Bailey's Irish Cream advertising offers a lifestyle not just a drink, as does Marks and Spencer's food marketing campaigns. The things we drink, eat, the places we stay, the events we attend become semiotic markers of how we are, or who we want to be, and a marker to the rest of the world what type of person we are.

Just as in the marketing of tourism and events, the marketing of food and hospitality draw on certain conventions that are shared across the semiotics of experience. The marketing of food and hospitality widely utilise what Johns and Pine (2002: 127) refer to as the 'authentic environments' of hospitality, the images used are empty of humans and modernity, they offer us an empty space in which we can search for the authentic. For example if you examine the marketing materials of Michelin starred restaurants such as Le Manoir aux Quat' Saisons offer a mediation on taste and gastronomy which define the preparation, social character, philosophy, aesthetics of food, the table, it identifies food and hospitality as art (Fantasia 1995). Its meaning is heightened by the juxtaposition of the images used in relation to the nature of fast food and the homogenisation of taste in contemporary society. This is semiotically reinforced by the representation of the vegetable gardens as it represents an organic means of production and authenticity, empty formal restaurants with classically laid tables, again free from signs of modernity and other customers, waiting staff etc.

The marketing of food and hospitality offers escape routes from everyday lived experience by its 'extraordinariness' and is differentiated from the routine and often unreflexive consumption of food as merely fuel (Marshall 2005). For example Pringle's 2011 campaign which defines their product as 90 pieces of fun, while icecream brands such as Haagen-Dazs or Magnum make a clear the link between food and sex. Hedonistic food marketing and the semiotics of experience creates a configuration of time and space which elevates the context of the food served to that of the extraordinary, think about how many times you see an advert in which someone eats something and is transported to another time or place. This is a convention that is widely used by luxury food items such as chocolate and soft drinks. This differentiation of time and space is also a recurrent theme in hospitality marketing, the use of empty restaurants, hotels, spas or swimming pools excluding temporal markers (people, cars, computers, telephone lines) is a semiotically constructed liminality within experience marketing that offers a '... cognitive imaginative and practical space in which everyone can access the things that mark off the social from the private' (Couldry 2001: 158). As such, the food and hospitality marketing creates a certain binary opposition to everyday lived experience (Kress and van Leeuwen 1996; Delind 2006), whereby the consumer is guided by embedded 'analytical processes' to place themselves within the image to become a part of the experience offered by the campaign. Although the sign vehicle's (marketing texts) symbolic authority

(Meyrowitz 1992; Couldry 2001) and representations direct the consumer towards an embedded 'signposted' definition of hospitality or food, the use of 'empty' landscapes creates a reflexive 'liminal' space, in which the consumer reflexively and hermeneutically interprets and projects personal meaning to the representations. The differentiation of time and space reinforces the significance of both the product and the experience.

The semiotic language of food and hospitality contained within marketing texts enables us to explore hospitality and food in terms of senses and the sensual, as an 'intimate frontier' (Dawkins 2009) in which we may locate the body. In other words the embedding of definitions of food and hospitality within marketing enables the individual to explore:

> the role of the sensual, the emotional, the expressive, for maintaining layered sets of embodied relationships to food and place.

(Delind 2006: 121)

Language of hospitality Semiotic themes	Language of food Semiotic themes
Escape	Extraordinary
Luxurious	Sophisticated
Service	Scientifically proven
Convenient	Sensuous
Timeless	Nutritious
Pamper	Celebration
Friendly	Fun
Timeless	Homemade/handmade
Historic	Authentic
Relax	Guilty pleasure
	Love and romance
	Passion
	Carnal
	Balanced and harmonious
	Moral and ethical

Figure 8.2: Sensual themes

The images used of food in both food and hospitality marketing elevate the food and dining experience to a level whereby it is so removed from real life that it can only be consumed vicariously (Magee 2007) and as a consequence creates a myth of food and the sensual or sexual (Reed-Danahay 1996). The embedding of hospitality and food is more than just shelter and food as fuel, it comes to represent a significant element in our lives and often we elevate hospitality, food preperation, dining practices, and eating to that of the extraordinary or even the sacred.

■ Austerity food marketing

Although the dominant discourse underpinning the semiotics of experience is defined by the notion of hedonistic food marketing, there is also another semiotic language of food that may be defined as 'austerity food marketing'. As a reaction to the increased awareness of the relationship between food choice and bad health and the rising levels of obesity, governments and organisations have invested in the development of a number of health campaigns, these provide a marketing message to change food choices, to resist unhealthy products or to cut the intake of certain ingredients. In order to facilitate these messages, a semiotics of austerity has been developed. It creates a new language of food that is removed from the semiotics of experience, as rather than focusing on experience focuses on consequence. It counters the semiotic language of food, ignores notions of luxury, escape and the sensual and replaces it with death, disease and threat. It places food back into the everyday, into the time and space of living and reminds us of our mortality. However, austerity food marketing faces many challenges as it draws upon a language that is not as persuasive or enticing as the others identified above. It also is a relatively new concept that is not as embedded as the other approaches outlined within this chapter, but what is significant is that it develops and utilises a language within marketing texts that attempts to challenge traditional

8

orthodoxies and approaches to the marketing of food. Conversely, it may be argued that its impact is limited because of the embedded nature of traditional forms of food marketing and the disparity in budgets between large multinational corporations selling fast food and those charged with promoting good health.

Language of food austerity Semiotic themes	
Risk	Less is more
Healthy	Wellness
Balance	Lifestyle
Abstinence	Surveillance
Loss	Self-governance
Risk Disease	Enemy
Exercise	Friend
Change	Harmony

Figure 8.3: Austerity themes

■ Semiotics and power

Semiosis and the process of signification is rarely innocent, this is especially the case when the semiotic script has a commercial base and motive. Unfortun ately this is often the stark reality of commercial marketing where the most economically beneficial meanings and signs are emphasised at the expense of those that are not. There may be exceptions to this rule – these mostly include those incidences and examples that align with the four pillars of sustainable marketing practice (see Chapter 9 for review of this conceptual normative framework) or social marketing generally. Accordingly all marketing materials and contexts can be examined for asymmetric power relations and power effects. For example, Schroeder and Zwick have examined the productive effects of advertising on gender and masculinity:

> Ad campaigns invoke gender identity, drawing their imagery primarily from the stereotyped iconography of masculinity and femininity. In this way, masculinity and femininity inter-

act smoothly with the logic of the market – advertising repre-sentations and consumption practices provide a meaningful system of difference, which has established strong limits to the possibilities of male and female consumer ontologies.

Going on to say:

Representations do not merely 'express' masculinity, rather, they play a central role in forming conceptions of masculinity and help construct market segments such as the New Man, playboys, connoisseurs, and lads, in the British vernacular.

(2004: 21–22)

In a similar way, the marketplace for food, and particularly advertising and packaging has been examined to reveal both their persuasive effects and influence, and their relationship to social and economic problems such as childhood obesity. Schor and Ford (2007: 137) for example, have argued that 'the increase of market-ing to children has coincided with significant deterioration in the healthfulness of children's diets, higher caloric intake and a rapid increase in rates of obesity and overweight'. They particularly focus on high caloric breakfast cereals and the effectiveness of symbolic appeals in advertising and package design. They argue that the use of cartoons and other attractive signs and symbols appear to make them 'cool' and incredibly attractive to their target audience.

Academics have also examined the semiotic framing of popula-tions and cultures generally and also the relationships between consumers and those involved in the production and staging of THEF experiences. For example Dann's (1996a) analysis of the people located within the tourism brochure illustrates the way in which local people are represented within marketing texts (see also Nelson 2005) and provides a good example of relationships and definitions of subordination and power relations. Seemingly subordination is reinforced in marketing texts like brochures by the angle, position or size of represented participants. This process is illustrated in SAGA Travellers' World Brochure which locates the visitor as guest, who is being served and entertained by a number of local musicians, thus representing difference in status and economic superiority. This is representative of a number of host/guest conventions and relationships that are continually utilised within the THEF marketing practice. Those aspects of a people or culture that have the greatest attractive properties and economic value are emphasised in the foreground while those that are not remain in the background or are lost. In a sense, marketing supports and reproduces cultural myths of people, places, and populations that have the greatest commercial value, they are the things that people want to see. In communicative staging of tourist experiences for instance, indigenous populations are often required to perform rituals and tribal acts such as dances for the pleasure of their audience. While this may have an economic return for the performer involved, an enduring consequence of this productive act is that it acts to blur fact from fiction simultaneously trivialising the history and culture of such people and places. For example in an evaluation of cultural tourism and performances in Bali, Picard (1990) argues that a central problem for the indigenous population is integration and access into the tourism industry. For those elements of the population who are willing to engage in performance for financial exchange it is argued that they become reliant, if not wholly dependent upon commercial intermediaries who negotiate their entry into the hotels and resorts where they perform. During negotiations, freedom of expression and agency maybe sacrificed. This seems the case when elements of the population and different dance troupes or performers are pitched against each other for contracts and the right to perform. As Picard explains:

> the commercial intermediaries, who are able to manipulate the competition between the different troupes, impose their own conditions, not only financially, but also in terms of the presentation of the spectacle and even the details of its program.
>
> (1990: 47–48)

This implication is shared in research by Middleton (2007) who has found that the staging of indigenous cultural performance as a tourism spectacle in Ecuador has similar effects and outcomes. Here dancers are seen to perform in clothing and artefacts that have no connection to their cultural history or past, such as tiger skins. Arguably then, such populations are reduced to economic actors in the script of a tourist spectacle of consumption, and authenticity and heritage become lost in this process and transformation.

As Kress and van Leeuwen state 'signs and images' and other representational practices such as communicative staging, (re) produce 'hierarchies of social power' (1996: 83). Thus, many of the semiotic structures and material practices identified in THEF marketing 'represent the world in hierarchical order' (1996: 85) and critically in which the relationship between the host – be it the culture, population or service personnel – and the consumer are identified. In a way the host is often represented as a servant or a cultural attraction and the visitor is consuming this through the marketing process and their experience.

The semiotics of THEF do not often reflect real or natural classifications, but rather they imply something. Examples of this can be seen in most forms of experience marketing and are important in giving significance to the language. From a semiotic and cultural perspective, marketing is not just an economic process it is also a significant and influential social and cultural practice. Not only can it create considerable good and value through creating wealth and constructing memorable and compelling consumer experiences it can also harm. Accordingly marketers should be conscious of the social order and reality that they are imposing on the marketplace and culture generally. It is our view that marketing practitioners should hold or develop a reflexive attitude that rests upon an informed view of the general process of semiosis and the unintentional effects of meaning production practices.

8

■ Conclusion

This chapter introduces the semiotics of experience and more significantly the semiotic language of tourism, hospitality, food and events. It also outlines a general theory of semiotics. The semiotics of experience play an important role in contemporary marketing practice. It underpins the marketing of experience, and raises questions as to how tourism, hospitality, food and events are presented and consumed, both within contemporary marketing texts and servicescapes. Quite often we do not take the time to understand the signs that are put in front of us, just like the traffic light example used earlier in the chapter, we merely accept that we have to stop. By taking the time to examine and analyse what images and other signifiers are being used in the staging of THEF, and what they mean and their effects we are better equipped as experience marketers. By undertaking this we can start to make sense of what people are looking for or seeking to avoid, in the sense of what motivates them or turns them off and what fuels and frames their desires and interactions with the marketplace. How the language of experience is constructed and how it can be used, it is also important to ask the question of what is missing, as this is as significant as what is included. It is also important to recognise that the meanings or conventions utilised within the semiotics of experience draw from a wide range of sources, therefore in order to understand the language we need to understand the social and cultural significance of the activity. We must learn the codes. Semiotics is not an exact science as it involves interpretation, and as such, everyone is going to interpret things in different ways, however we can identify the elements that we can all agree on.

9 Ethics, Sustaina... Marketing and the Green Consumer

■ Introduction

There is a growing trend within marketing to work towards a more sustainable agenda, in which the ethics of both the production, dissemination and consumption of marketing materials is becoming increasingly questioned. Sustainability has been a significant theme in THEF for a number of years, there is a long traditional of sustainable tourism experiences that range from trekking in undeveloped areas to visiting Center Parcs, while food production has developed clear links with the 'Fairtrade', organic and slow food movements. Meanwhile organisations such as Marriott Hotels have invested heavily in their green credentials and large events such as Glastonbury Music Festival have their foundations in raising money for charities. As such the notion of sustainability has become one of the central themes to experiences marketing and has seen the emergence of the green consumer. The theme of sustainability within experiences marketing can be seen to fulfil a number of objectives that can be broadly divided into two elements, the first is where sustainability is used as a means of product differentiation, adding to the brand value, reinforcing the credentials of the organisation, impacting on buyer choice. In other words it adds an economic value to the company's or organisation's product. The second element is the impact the notion of sustainability has on the consumer's perception of products, how it makes us feel and ultimately how it makes us behave. This chapter will examine the greening of marketing has on THEF marketing.

The greening of experiences marketing

It is argued that current marketing practices have failed the sustainability agenda (Mitchell and Saren 2008), this failure may be seen to be the direct result of the paradox that exists between marketing and the concept of sustainability, marketing is fundamentally a commercial activity that encourages people to buy products, to purchase things they do not need or require, as Kotler states that marketing is:

> ...a social and managerial process by which individuals and groups obtain what they need and want through creating and exchanging products and value with others.

> (2008: 7)

As stated previously experiences marketing needs to be understood as being different from other forms of marketing and as such, the above quote needs to also include the social and cultural practices that underpin the production and consumption of food, tourism, events and hospitality, and the impacts that occur within the generating and represented society and culture. Parsons and Maclaren (2009: 14) summarise the criticism of marketing as 'fuelling consumption and encouraging materialism by stimulating wants as a means of satisfying human needs'. Sustainability on the other hand, is underpinned by notions of anti-consumerism, sensitive development and not encouraging waste etc. *Our Common Future* (Brundtland Commission 1987) provides one of the most useful and widely used definitions of what is meant be sustainability, the report defines sustainability as 'meeting the needs of the present without depleting resources or harming natural cycles for future generations'. As marketers we have to reconcile this paradox and question our role within the global economy. As Mitchell and Saren state:

> The philosophy of marketing speaks the language of material possession, individuality, and newness, and works on the assumption of unlimited growth and the accumulation of waste.
>
> (2008: 399)

Thus, every time we promote a form of food, destination event etc. we enter into the commercial world and as such our behaviour has an impact upon communities, individuals or hosts, sometimes this is positive and sometimes it is negative. However, all of this makes the assumption that notions of morality and rationality is a given, and that all organisations and consumers are concerned about their ethical footprint (Moisander and Pesonen 2002).

However there has been a growing movement by companies to adopt or to be seen to adopt more sustainable practices and for many companies these form the basis of many campaigns (Mitchell and Saren 2008). For example Starbucks and Cadbury's have used their association with 'Fairtrade' as the core message of the campaign, while McDonald's have focused on the zero additives in their products. This approach not only enables them to attempt to maintain their market position but also it further develops the brand value of their companies. This is reflected in the Chartered Institute of Marketing developing an Ethics and Social Responsibility Section within their resources. They go on to state that:

> The role of the marketer these days could be seen in terms of connecting with stakeholders not only in terms of value, but in terms of values. In a world where intangible assets and corporate reputation are centre stage, the marketing team needs to focus on ethical issues more than ever before.
>
> (CIM 2010)

This movement within the marketing industry is not purely motivated by philanthropic actions, but has its foundation in maximising profit or protecting your market position or in marketing speak the 'Triple Bottom Line'. The CIM declare that the Triple Bottom Line:

> …creates a framework for companies to become sustainable without ignoring the importance of the financial bottom line and other concerns that are vital to a company's survival, growth and economic success.

> (2007:5)

This raises the question as to what is exactly meant by the phrase or concept of sustainability in marketing. Is the sustainability movement just an aspect of marketing that has provided a new dimension to the formulation of marketing strategies? (Mitchell and Saren 2008) or is it a social and cultural movement that has infiltrated contemporary marketing practices. It is clear however that experiences marketing utilises and has developed a relationship to the sustainable movement that differs from other areas of marketing.

Experiences marketing utilises the notion of sustainability and ethical marketing differently from Social Marketing. Social Marketing utilises marketing and advertising to reduce consumption, waste etc. (see Peattie and Peattie 2009), and can often be seen as de-marketing the product and often is encouraging anti-consumption, for example the campaigns that are used to encourage healthy eating, reduction in salt in-take or anti-smoking. However, representations of the sustainability or ethical within experiences marketing incorporates the ethical or green element into the product, is it may be argued that it is encouraging consumption, but consumption in a more sympathetic or informed manner, but is core to the tourism, food, hospitality or event experience. It becomes the experience and 'enculturates' (Kozinets, Handelman & Lee 2010) the experience with cultural capital and confirms its cultural credentials as a form of consumption. This is quite a significant distinction as the motivation, consequences and significance of advertisement will depend upon how we contextualise the product. For example in the case of the social marketing campaigns that encourage us to eat five pieces of fresh fruit and vegetables in order improve our health, this to a certain degree is motivated by an anti-marketing sentiment as it is attempting to stop us consuming processed or fast food. It is selling an ideal thus it is not commoditising the food, but attempting to change behaviour. However, if we see a vegetarian dish that forms part of an advert for a Michelin starred restaurant, and is essentially healthy as it contains part of our 'Five a Day' vegetable and fruit intake, even the healthy becomes elevated to that of the sacred or hedonistic as the humble vegetable is elevated to the level of the extraordinary. There has been a growing agenda of integrating the natural environment into the business agendas and practices and a common corporate objective (see Mitchell and Saren 2008 for interesting discussion on sustainable marketing). In short, THEF marketing is a commercial process that uses sustainable or green experiences as a element of the experience. Experiences marketing thus commodifies notion of ethical consumption, sustainability and greening, it encourages consumption. On the other hand, social marketing does not encourage consumption, it encourages austerity and denial of excess. Thus sustainable or green tourism is not anti-marketing, but it is selling us the experience of being considerate or ethical, it becomes the product, that is aimed at a particular market segment and generates income or profit. However, we cannot ignore the significance of sustainable or green marketing as a driving force in contemporary THEF marketing, and as such, it is important that we understand the debates that surround sustainable that informs contemporary THEF marketing practices.

■ Defining sustainability

Sustainability in its purest form may be seen as an ideological and idealistic concept in which exploitation of people, landscapes, countries, cultures and peoples is eradicated. In social marketing literature, green consumer behaviour has been viewed as a form of ethically orientated consumer behaviour that is motivated not only by personal needs, but also for the concern of the welfare of society and the environment (see Mosiander and Pesonen 2002). However as we live in a society that is dominated by commerce the best we can hope to create is a workable definition that offers some form of workable compromise. The best way of understanding sustainability is to think of sustainability as the roof that straddles a building and is held up by four pillars (see Figure 9.1). When we are assessing or making judgements about the values of a brand or, the sustainability of the product we need to make judgements on how sustainable the product or experience is in terms of its social, cultural, economic or environmental credentials, it is these four pillars upon which sustainability sits. If we ignore one or two of these pillars then the whole concept of sustainability collapses. When analysing the way in which experiences marketing approaches sustainability we often find that it concentrates on only one of the pillars rather than all four with economic sustainability driving the company at the cost of overlooking the other elements.

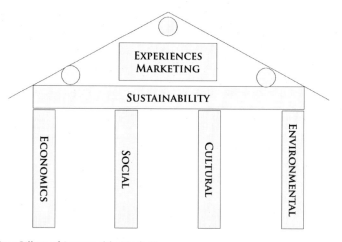

Figure 9.1: The Four Pillars of Sustainable Marketing

In order to analyse sustainable marketing it is important that we understand how experiences marketing is related to and influences our relationship with the THEF experiences, and the debates that underpin the marketing and promotion of experiences and destinations as this determines what we mean by sustainability and how we utilise the concept in contemporary marketing practices. There is increasing pressure on companies and marketers to adopt a more ethical or sustainable approach to their marketing practices, traditionally these issues have been located within the discussion surrounding the ability of the sovereign consumer to filter information and to make judgements utilising their own value systems, rather than being persuaded by marketing to consume unethical or non-sustainable products. Thus marketers are not responsible for consumption patterns or consumer behaviour as it is the consumer who has made their informed choice. This approach in normative marketing has traditionally let the sector off the hook, as it distance itself from the actual act of production and consumption. As such we need to consider the that experiences marketing is complicit in promoting the consumption of experiences that may have negative social or cultural impacts and without the effective marketing or commodification of experiences that impact may not have occurred. Ultimately marketers are central to the process and as such need to accept and take responsibility for their actions.

■ Social sustainability

■ Social inclusion and exclusion

Marketing is both inclusive and exclusive, some people are invited into the consumption experience while others become excluded because of their social position, demographic status or the fact that they make up part of the society that is being marketed in experience marketing texts. For example, if you examine how local people are represented in tourism brochures they are seen as either providing service or are represented as an attraction (Dann 1996a). This simple distinction identifies power relations and who has the economic superiority within societies, the local or host society becomes excluded from the marketing experience. Thus,

9

experiences marketing define social relationships and come to represent contemporary power relations between the First and the Third World, the North or the South or even the Provincial and the Urban. Marketing comes to represent the world in which we live.

■ Marketing defines social relationships

The use of identified language, images and referents are determined by positioning, and segmentation within experiences marketing texts. However, this process makes assumption about the social and cultural position and knowledge of the consumer. It includes and excludes consumers according to their social knowledge/position and represents the power relations that surround contemporary consumer relations by distributing and awarding power.

■ Cultural sustainability

■ Cultural commodification

The use of cultural images, cultural production or cultural events often form the basis of experiences marketing campaigns. The consumption of culture whether in the form of an event or activity is often one of the major motivating factors in the consumer's decision making process, as such culture becomes a commodity to be bought, sold and consumed as part of the touristic or leisure process. However, any form of culture represents its generating culture, it represents the very essence of who we are, people have fought and died to protect and defend their cultural autonomy and freedom to produce elements of their own culture. As such, the representation or commodification within experiences marketing needs to be treated in a sensitive and sustainable manner. Often there is little concern about protecting or representing culture in a manner that reduces it to its lowest common denominator, in which images and text remove the activity from its cultural context and which communicate that culture to rest of the world.

■ Marketing and cultural representation

The images and words that form marketing campaigns and adverts create a story that makes up our understanding of the world, and in particular it makes up part of a historical discourse that informs how we define people, places and their culture. Thus, there is a significant amount of power in the ability to define and make judgements about culture. This power becomes elevated in experiences marketing as tourism brochures and food advertisements commodify culture as one of the central themes that are seen to attract consumers in search of escape, authenticity or something extraordinary that cannot be found in their own culture. For example, think about how we define countries such as Australia, often our first thoughts are the Outback, Aboriginal people or art. Many of these images are defined by our relationship to brochures, adverts or travel programmes. It is an idealistic view of Australia that removes culture from the realities of everyday, or the struggles that Aboriginal people face in a modern world. As a consequence, as marketers we have a responsibility to think about the impact marketing has on the cultures we are representing, how the consumer may interpret these and what it says about that culture. This responsibility forms one of the significant elements of the notion of sustainability forwarded within this chapter.

■ Economic sustainability

■ Marketing in a capitalist world

The debates that surround the notion of sustainability within normative marketing often focuses on the financial or economic impact, of how to sustain market share or turnover. This is not surprising as one of the fundamental purposes of marketing is to create wealth, economic value is omnipotent (Firat and Dholakia 1998). However, as part of the sustainability/ethics debate we need to own up to the reality of the marketing process and to recognise that as an economic activity, there has to be an exchange of goods and services, and that surplus is made by utilising the resources of others. What this does is to locate marketing in the debate that recognises the essential asymmetries that exist within both the production and consumption of experiences, but also in the economic system in which it is located. The global nature of tourism and hospitality and food production often relies on the relationship between developed and less developed countries and that developed economies utilise the resources (cheap labour, minerals, coffee, cocoa, culture, food, landscapes, rivers, beaches etc.) of less developed countries, and that by processing or utilising the resource a profit or surplus can be made. This can clearly be demonstrated by analysing the relationship between globalisation debates and the hospitality industry.

■ The economy of hospitality

Hospitality is part of a large globalised industry and can be used to illustrate how globalisation creates an economic inequality between developed and less developed countries or economies. For example, a hotel may be developed in Kenya, cheap labour is used to build it, it is then furnished by importing beds, carpets from a central depot that may be in the UK, leading to negative exports for the receiving country, the larders are then stocked with European or American beer and liquor, managerial staff are usually expatriates, all of this leads to the income not entering Kenya. The impact of this is that the country needs to generate foreign exchange in order to generate income and bring wealth to the country, however as goods are imported, the income generated by tourists leaves the country and impacts upon the country's balance of payments. So although the solution may be financially sustainable for the hotel, this may not be the case for the country whose resources are supporting the enterprise.

The marketing of food, events, hospitality and tourism reinforces the global relations between host and guest, and organisations which creates a formal duty of care that for many years was ignored. However many large companies have recognised that they have a social responsibility, and should not merely exploit developing country's resources whether this be extracting minerals for mobile phones, or the use of poorly paid labour to produce footballs and football kits. This approach to corporate responsibility can be seen to make good business sense and can directly positively inform consumer behaviour in choice of informing choice or reinforcing consumer loyalty. Thus, to act sustainably and ethically can make good business sense as it builds a relationship between the producer and consumer.

■ The green consumer

There appears to have been the emergence of new category of consumer whose purchasing behaviour is motivated by how ethical or sustainable the product they are buying is. This concern can be seen as a direct result of the excesses of globalisation and mass production or consumption, and perhaps fulfils a need for something that is more authentic and simple. Over the past decade there has been a huge increase in the number of products that fall into this category, whether it is organic food, sustainable or green tourism or ethically sourced coffee or chocolate. Moisander recognises that:

> environment-friendly consumption may be characterized as a highly complex form of consumer behaviour, both intellectually and morally as well as in practice.

> (2007: 1)

Significantly, our awareness of sustainable approaches to consumption and our purchasing habits are endowed with high levels of cultural capital. This cultural capital is used by THEF consumers to distinguish themselves from other consumers by using the moral dimensions of green consumerism as an 'aesthetic of existence' or 'art of existence' (Moisander and Pesonen 2002: 330). 'Sustainable' or 'eco' are reflected in certain forms of consumer behaviour that

9

include impacts that are informed by the moral discourses of 'making a difference, voluntary simplicity and radical environmentalism' (Moisander and Pesonen 2002).

■ There is a great deal of evidence that if we have the choice of two similar products at a similar price but one is organic, sustainable or green we would be more likely to choose that product. Thus, by adopting a sustainable approach to the production and management practices, it will often promote positive buying practices by consumers. Therefore, being green makes good business sense and is becoming an increasingly significant in underpinning brand values and brand equity.

■ A hedonistic response to the consumption of green or sustainable products; as individuals we find joy in doing something good, thus our hedonistic pleasure from eating an organic or 'Fair Trade' chocolate bar becomes heighted as we enjoy it at the gustatory level and at the philosophical level.

Consumers are also becoming more militant in their consumer behaviour, and take direct action by boycotting products that have been unearthed as unethical or damaging to the environment. For example, Nike came under a great deal of criticism for their production methods and utilising cheap or child labour in developing countries and this led directly to a boycotting of their products (Eckhardt *et al.* 2010). The result of this consumer behaviour forced Nike and many of their competitors to change their production practices (see Kozinets, Handelman & Lee 2010 for discussion on anti-consumption). Similar concerns have previously been raised about Nestlé's alleged use of palm oil in Kit Kats (Hickman 2010) and Sainsbury's sourcing of GM-reared cows in their products (see BBC 2004). It is also interesting to look at the work of pressure groups such as Tourism Concern (www.tourismconcern.org. uk) who encourage and organise direct action to counteract the pressures of globalisation on less developed countries and fragile habitats.

Companies are increasingly changing their stance and relationship to sustainable or ethical sourcing of materials and management approaches. This approach often forms a significant element in the retention of customer's strategy and in turn protecting market share. Companies such as Starbucks, Cadbury's and Marriott (Euro RSG 2010) have used their green credentials as a central element in their current marketing campaigns.

It can be argued that consumers' relationship to sustainably or ethically produced products is more than a trend or fashion, but rather it has come to represent the foundations of a cultural movement and an identifiable demographic whose lives are informed by the green and sustainable movement. The uncertainties of the post-industrial society coupled with the search for simplicity and authenticity of experience that is presented in television shows such as *River Cottage* and *Jamie at Home* informs the consumers' search for the sustainably and ethical practices that become part of everyday lived experiences. Experiences marketing again utilises the theme to create and promise an experience that will make you feel good in a hedonistic way and good in a value driven/philosophical way. Yet in normative marketing terms the green consumer forms an identifiable target market that is generally well educated and relatively affluent and most important, is searching for the 'good life' within contemporary consumerism. However, for some authors such as Eckhardt *et al.*, the ethical or green consumer may be seen as merely a myth, in identifying the consumer's relationship and understanding of ethical consumption patterns they state:

> Economic rationalization focuses on consumers wanting to get the most value for their money, regardless of their ethical beliefs. Institutional dependency refers to the belief that institutions such as the government are responsible to ethically regulate what produces can be sold (and).... That some unethical behaviours on the part of corporations must exist in order for macro level economic development to occur.

> (2010: 426)

As such, although consumers may have ambitions to change their purchasing patterns by purchasing more green or ethically sourced products they are 'ultimately blinded by the seduction of consumer goods' (Devinney 2010) and that although they may wish to be seen as caring they ignore social and environmental issues as they purchase the products, brands and services they are loyal to (Eckhardt *et al.* 2010). Nevertheless, marketing continues to utilise the green and ethical discourse to underpin marketing campaigns and attribute the desire to consume ethically as part of the characteristics of various identified segment groups.

■ Sustainable approaches to tourism

Although the Green Consumer may be categorised as an identifiable habitus or consumption group, it is particularly sophisticated. The analyse of the impacts of tourism has a long and rich tradition (Swarbrook 1998; Inskeep 1991; Neto 2002), this has resulted in a complex debate that can be discussed in some depth and has resulted in both the analysis of the sector and the identification of a niche. For example Euro RSG (2010: 3) identify the following categories of green tourism experiences:

- **Flashpacking:** Backpacking with flash or style; travel that combines modest accommodation with free spending on activities and other indulgences; budget backpacking that incorporates high-end technology.

- **Geotourism:** Tourism that sustains or enhances the character of a place – its environment, heritage, aesthetics, culture – and the well-being of its residents.

- **Rough Lux:** Luxury experiences that incorporate time for reflection and personal encounters with people, nature, and architecture, as well as food and social and cultural experiences linked to geographic locations.

- **Staycation:** A vacation spent at home or nearby.

- **Slow travel:** Travel that provides an opportunity to become part of local life and to connect to a place, its people, and its culture.

- **Voluntourism:** Voluntary service experiences that include travel to a destination in order to realise one's service intentions; the conscious, seamlessly integrated combination of voluntary service to a destination with the traditional elements of travel and tourism (arts, culture, geography, history, and recreation).

What this recognises is that there are various categories and levels of greenness, this follows through into food, events, hospitality and tourism and that as consumers we position ourselves within experiences that meet our definitions of authenticity and the simplistic.

■ Green marketing and the process of greenwashing

The inclusions of a company's green credentials within both their marketing campaigns, their mission and values statements are becoming increasingly common and often forms the unique selling point of a product. The marketing of food and tourism in particular often utilise green discourses to underpin marketing campaigns, with banner claims about the ethical, sustainable or organic nature of their products. However, often these claims are not investigated, or there is little proof provided to substantiate the green statements, yet often we are willing to accept them without question as it eases our conscience about being a consumer. For Alves:

> Green marketing is the tactical instrument by which companies derive value from Corporate Social Responsibility (CSR): hyping their green credentials in a poorly regulated environment where most claims cannot be corroborated.

> (2009: 3)

However, claims of being green or ethical are often overstated and in certain cases just untrue. Greenpeace define greenwashing as:

> ...the act of misleading consumers regarding the environmental practices of a company or the environmental benefits of a product or service.

(Gallicano 2011: 1)

The concept of greenwashing appeared as pressure groups and individuals began to identify inconsistencies between companies' claims and their actual behaviour. For example Romero (2008) analyses the work of Jay Westeveld who in the 1980s recognised the trend for hotels to encourage customers to reuse towels and bedding, yet they did not have recycling policies, and as such, the policy for reuse was motivated by cost cutting rather than environmental concerns or ethical behaviour. It is clear that consumers are motivated and influenced by the green debate, yet often this desire to engage in ethical or sustainable consumption has been adopted by marketers as an effective strategy to sell their products more successfully.

Alves (2009: 5) identifies that there are six common sins of greenwashing and green marketing that inform contemporary marketing practices, these include the:

- **Sin of the Hidden Trade-off:** Whereby a product is deemed green as the result of one attribute, for example where the packaging is recyclable, but the contents is not or in the terms of sustainable tourism, the holiday may be sustainable but the flights to the destination are not.

- **Sin of No Proof:** Companies will make green claims without them being substantiated by a third party. For example there are many companies claiming their foods are produced in an ethical manner, but unless they are accredited by organizations such as 'Fairtrade' or the 'Soil Association' there is little proof.

- **Sin of Vagueness:** The messages contained within advertisements are often very vague or obscure, for example packaging maybe labelled as recyclable, however this often only relates to 10 per cent of the entire packaging. Phrases such 'ethically sourced', 'free range' or 'benefits the local community' also fit into this category of sin.

- **Sin of Irrelevance:** Companies will forward attributes such as the product being biodegradable, yet the product may never have been harmful in the first place. A similar example is the claim that the packaging is CFC free, yet it has been illegal to produce packaging containing it since the 1970s.

- **Sin of Lesser of Two Evils:** This involves offering the consumer a product that is harmful to the planet but appears to be less so than alternative versions. For example hybrid cars which still produce carbon emissions when they are being built and driven, but are marketed as environmentally friendly. There is also a strong trend in food to make claims about levels of fat being reduced, but often this is compensated with higher levels of salt or sugar to give taste. Or chips/crisps that have no 'transfats' or 'MSGs' but are still bad for your health.

- **Sin of Fibbing:** Finally some companies just lie about their green credentials.

Alves also quotes research undertaken by TerraChoice Environmental Marketing in 2007 which claimed that 1017 out of 1018 green-marketed products committed at least one of these sins and, with over 50 per cent of the products committing the sin of hidden trade-off.

As stated previously, there is still a concern that green practices as CSR policies are motivated by saving money (Bivins 2009; Gallicano 2011), or are for its branding, public relations, and legal value (Alves 2009) rather than the planet. However, through marketing practices, organisations have been able to promote themselves as 'environmental stewards' as they provide very little in-depth information or transparency regarding their operations and business practices (Lyon and Maxwell 2006), and that in reality, little is being done to protect the environment despite the claims they make in their marketing (Bivins 2009). This raises questions as to the obligations and responsibilities of companies to be transparent, Rawlins (2009) provides guidelines for this:

1 Companies must present accurate, substantial and relevant information.

2 Companies should liaise with stakeholders to discover what type of information they require.

3 Companies must provide objective and balanced data about policies and activities.

Rawlins defines these guidelines as providing 'substantial completeness' whereby 'a reasonable person's requirements for information are satisfied' (2009: 74). If we are to adopt a sustainable or ethical approach to marketing it is important that the industry adopts an approach to green marketing that is truthful and transparent. The debate surrounding the 'sovereign consumer' rests on the precept that the consumer is provided with all the information and they reflexively make the purchase or behavioural decision as a result of interpreting and analysing the provided data. If the information is not clear, transparent, appropriate or true, then the defence of the sovereign consumer is negated and as marketers we become culpable for some of the inequalities, health problems and environmental damage that exists in the world in which we inhabit.

■ Conclusion

The relationship between sustainable and ethical practices and marketing is a complex one that is tied up in many of the debates such as consumer behaviour, choice and power forwarded in this book. The use of sustainability and the ethical approaches or themes within THEF marketing provides us with an interesting paradox, which is different from the tradition definition of sustainability with normative marketing practices. Sustainable and ethical marketing is becoming an increasingly popular element of experiences marketing and can be seen to present two very different messages which is 'sustainability as product' and 'sustainability as non-consumption', both are part of experiences marketing, but each offer very different experiences. The green consumer as presented within this chapter is also a complicated construct who is motivated by various experiences and products, each consumer being driven by their own motivations whether those be to increase cultural capital, to belong to a particular habitus or to behave in the most ethical and sustainable way possible. To be truly sustainable is not to consume at all, however in the consumer orientated world in which we live and the continual search for hedonistic experiences, the best we can hope to achieve is some form of light green consumption patterns. This chapter also encourages us as marketers, and as consumers, to think about the role of marketing in commoditising and promoting societies, cultures, history, heritage, produce and environment as part of the economic system rather than adopting cynical greenwashing tactics to hide or mask the nature or impact of our product upon both individuals and the environment. Marketing fuels desires creates wants and searches for products to generate wealth, it is no good to merely argue that governments or that the sovereign consumer is ultimately responsible for any impacts through their freedom to choice. Marketing, needs to be accountable and ultimately ethical, whether this possible in a consumerist capitalist society, is highly debatable and is ultimately the product of your own and the marketing industry's conscience.

9

10 Conclusion: a manifesto for critical marketing in THEF

■ Introduction

This book has developed a critical approach to marketing in tourism, hospitality, events and food. As stated previously, the work developed here should be used to complement traditional approaches that will be found in most generic marketing texts. This book was motivated by the recognition that although there is a growing body of work that takes a critical approach to THEF experiences, there is no text that brings together these debates into a coherent piece of work. This concluding chapter provides an overview of the book and what may be seen as a manifesto for the critical marketing movement in THEF.

■ A journey into critical marketing

The structure of this book was developed to introduce and develop the reader's knowledge of the debates that underpin critical marketing in the THEF sectors. The adoption of a multidisciplinary approach has enables the analysis of marketing as a management, social, cultural, economic and individual process and practice. The chapter structure and content was constructed in a manner so as to develop a progression in the understanding and knowledge of marketing in the THEF arena. It is possible to organise the chapters into three distinct but overlapping debates, these were:

■ Understanding experience and the consumer (Chs. 2–4)

This part first located and explored the experience of THEF, how and why it is so significant for the individual consumer, and how its significance has become embedded socially, culturally and historically. Chapter 2 enables the reader or practitioner to understand their sector and how this differs from other consumer experiences. Chapters 3 and 4 take a more practical approach to locating the critical considerations developed in this book within the traditional approaches and debates that dominate and structure contemporary practices. This is important as the themes developed in this book need to work alongside and complement this traditional approach to marketing. Chapter 4 identifies the various types of resources that impact upon the way in which the individual consumer relates to THEF products, experiences and marketing practices, this is key in developing the concept that all consumers are individuals with differing desires, needs and wants. In conclusion, this section sets up the debates that permeate throughout the book and recognise that an interdisciplinary and holistic approach to marketing can create effective and insightful practices.

■ The consumer as individual (Chs 5–8)

This part explores the individual's relationship to the product, the consumption process and how they negotiate marketing practices. Just as the first part located the THEF product or experience, this part locates the consumer at the centre of marketing practice. Chapter 5 explores how the consumer selects, acquires and consumes products and experiences within the marketing process. It also examines the various personal factors that inform this, as a consequence this engagement with marketing and THEF becomes a variable and very personal project. This theme is further developed in Chapter 6 which analyses how the individual's knowledge of products and

10

experiences, and their consumption patters are used by others and themselves to locate and identify them with a particular group or habitus', thus the way in which the consumer engages with THEF becomes a marker of their identity and membership of a particular class of consumer or tribe. This chapter identifies that the consumption process is not just concerned with physical consumption but is imbued with other social and cultural practices. The remaining two chapters in this section are concerned with understanding how the individual consumer interprets, negotiates, resists and finds meaning within THEF marketing. Chapter 7 presents a discussion that identifies how as individuals we interpret the world in which we live and recognises that many influencing factors such as our value systems or life biography will result in each consumer interpreting marketing practices and communication in individual and creative ways, and as a result we cannot make the assumption that everyone will find meaning in products in the same way. This theme is further developed in Chapter 8 by exploring the semiotics of marketing, this chapter explores how meaning is transferred from the marketer to the consumer through the use of signs and semiotic conventions. This chapter draws on the previous six chapters as all of the information about product and the individual become manifested in what may be termed a semiotic language of THEF. This part is of particular importance as it enables us to understand how the individual finds meaning and how we communicate with them in an efficient and creative manner while recognising that each consumer is a free-thinking, reflexive individual.

■ The marketer as moral guardian (Chs 9–10):

The final two chapters in this book develop the theme of ethical and sustainable marketing in the THEF sector. If you break down the THEF product, although we are selling experiences to the consumer, what we are in fact selling is people's culture, society, traditions, environment and natural resources. All of these are very fragile and once damaged or destroyed it is very difficult to repair or replace them. As marketers we have a responsibility to behave and operate in an ethical and sustainable manner. However, as marketing is located within a competitive and commercial world, it is often at odds with this assertion. Chapter 9 explores the notion of ethics, sustainability within the THEF sector, while this chapter presents a manifesto for THEF practices that responds to some of the concerns highlighted in the previous chapter.

The purpose of this book has been to create a critical framework in which the marketing of THEF experiences may be located. As this is one of the first texts that attempts to do this, the authors feel that it is important that we present what may be seen as a manifesto for the marketing of THEF. This manifesto lays out an agenda and philosophical discourse that should both influences traditional marketing practices and stimulate debate in the THEF marketing community.

■ A Manifesto for THEF Marketing: The five precepts of critical marketing

Precept 1

That marketing needs to be understood as a social and cultural activity that surrounds the world of commerce and which frames the needs, wants, desires and goals of consumers in the THEF sector. The result of this is to place the consumer at the centre of the marketing process. Consequently this is to move away from an over-reliance on economic and psychological theory and notions of exchange that are expressed in the positivistic marketing tradition and to adopt an approach which effectively utilises both positivistic and interpretivistic modes of enquiry.

Precept 2

As expressed in Chapter 2, it must be recognised that THEF needs to be located in a very particular and specific context as it is sig-

10

nificant at the social and cultural level, as well as at the level of the individual consumer – THEF is used as markers of the consumers' lives and expressions of their social identity. The upshot of this for the marketer is that they must take a multidisciplinary approach so that they can truly understand the significance of their sector. It is only once that this has been achieved that we can engage effectively in the practice and process of marketing THEF experiences.

Precept 3

In recognising the multidisciplinary nature of marketing within the THEF sector, marketers should be equipped with a broadened view of this practice and process. Namely, they should develop a commercially significant repertoire that not only includes the exchange perspective of marketing, but also incorporates the service and interaction perspective that recognises the significance of marketing as a cultural process and practice. This will allow marketers to recognise the significance and influence of what they presently do, which is arguably framed within the exchanged view. They also need to recognise the significant agentic properties and nature of their consumers and marketing audience. Consumers are not merely the target that present dominant approaches to marketing tend to view them as, they are incredibly adept at shaping the meanings, value and values that are provided by THEF products, activities and services. Marketers should therefore widen their viewpoint and practices to allow for the cultural expressions and projects of their consumers and target markets. This view is expressed in Chapters 5 and 6, whereby we recognise and develop the notion that consumers cannot merely by seen as part of a homogeneous segment but that we need to recognise each individual's motivations, values and ambitions. Additionally, it is important to accept that there has been a restructuring of society in which society and group membership is not defined by class or economic income but rather by cultural and consumer knowledge, practices and experience. The result of this is that we can not simplistically place individuals in one market segment as they are dynamic and reflexive. What is more we also must recognise that people can and do belong to more than one consumer group and can/will happily flit between them without experiencing any disorientation or discomfort. In fact this juxtaposition of styles and patterns of consumption will arguably be celebrated and embraced (Firat and Dholakia 2006).

Precept 4

There has been a long tradition in marketing that carries an assumption that the consumer does not resist or questions marketing authority (see Holt 2002 for review) and that, we as marketers, do not question how the consumer finds meaning or relates to marketing communication or practices. As such there has been an assumption of a singular worldview or consumer reality. In contrast to this, by accepting and understanding that the consumer interprets and negotiates marketing and how and why they do this, a marketer of THEF expereinces is better able to reflect the worldview and reality of consumers and design products and experiences which better match and fit into their lives. This reinforces the need to adopt a more qualitative approach towards developing marketing strategies and approaches. Not only do we need to account for a consumer's worldview or ontology when trying to understand our marketing audiences we also need to consider the elements that support or constrain their choices and which also frame the outcomes of their consumption. Consumers come to the market equipped with their own unique range and quota of resources. Whilst marketing has always recognised the significance of a consumer's socio-economic status and its relationship to a segments propensity to consume, it has previously neglected the range of other allocative resources which consumers deploy when consuming goods, services and activities. Accordingly, THEF marketers should seek to get closer to their consumers on what can be described as a micro level to try to understand how material objects and other resources such as time and space, create opportunities both for consumers and marketers to create valuable and meaningful experiences. Equally, on a more

10

critical level, we must recognise how apparent deficiencies in these resources may subject consumers to significant disadvantages or place them in the way of harm.

Precept 5

It is no longer acceptable to use the sovereign consumer clause as an excuse for the excesses of marketing. As global citizens, marketers should and must take responsibility for their actions and approaches. The adoption of ethical and sustainable approaches should be at the core of all of our activities, and should be at the top of the marketer's tool box. Sustainable marketing should not be a bolt-on to the traditional approach to marketing in the sectors, instead it should be an overarching value that feeds into all marketing strategies and approaches. This is of particular significance within the THEF sectors as we are promoting and selling the environment, people's cultures, their history and their natural and physical resources. What is more, in many cases we are also promoting, producing and staging ludic and hedonic pleasures that if taken to the excess can lead to personal, social and economic harm. Sustainability should be there to protect and preserve not as a marketing commodity to be packaged and sold.

■ Conclusion

This book provides an introduction to critical marketing in THEF, and should only be seen as a starting point for the reader. Although critical marketing is often criticised for its lack of empirical data or its purely theoretical foundations or approaches, it can be argued that adopting such an approach can enhance practice. If the result of engaging in the debates that surround critical marketing result in the reader or practitioner understanding the significance of their sector, and what they are selling, and understanding what wants, needs, desires and motivations their target consumers have then surely this must make the marketer more efficient in their everyday professional lives. Additionally, the adoption of a more sensitive approach to marketing does not only attract consumers it ensures that they have a product to promote and sell in the future. In short, traditional marketing approaches are demonstrably important and successfully engage customers, this book argues that a critical approach will serve to enhance this by making marketing more creative, reflexive, and efficient.

10

Bibliography

Albers, P.C. and James, W.R. (1988) 'Travel photography: a methodological approach', *Annals of Tourism Research* **15**, 134–158.

Alexander, A. (2000) 'Codes and contexts: practical semiotics for the qualitative researcher', *Market Research Society Annual Conference*, http://www.semioticsolutions.com/ref.aspx?id=78

Allen, D. and Anderson, F. (1994) 'Consumption and social stratification: Bourdieu's distinction', *Advances in Consumer Research* **21**, 70–74.

Althusser, L. (1971) *Lenin and Philosophy and Other Essays*, New York: Monthly Review Press.

Alves, I. (2009) 'Green spin everywhere: how greenwashing reveals the limits of the CSR paradigm', *Journal of Global Change and Governance* **II** (I), winter/spring.

Anderson, J. (1993) 'The role of interpretation in communication theory', in *Verbo-visual Literacy*, Symposium of the International Visual Literacy Association, Delphi, June 25-29.

Arnould, E. (2005) 'Animating the big middle', *Journal of Retailing* **81** (2), 89–96.

Arnould, E., Price, L. and Tierney, P. (1998) 'Communicative staging of the wilderness servicescape', *Services Industries Journal* **18** (3), 90–115.

Arnould, E.J. and Price, L.L. (1993) 'River magic: extraordinary experience and the extended service encounter', *Journal of Consumer Research* **20** (1), 24–45.

Arnould, E.J. and Thompson, C.J. (2005) 'Consumer culture theory (CCT): twenty years of research', *Journal of Consumer Research* **31** (4), 868–882.

Arnould, E.J., Price, L.L. and Otnes, C. (1999) 'Making magic consumption', *Journal of Contemporary Ethnography* **28** (1), 33–68.

Arnould, E.J. Price, L.L. and Malshe, A. (2006) 'Toward a cultural resource-based theory of the consumer', in R.F. Lusch and S.L. Vargo (eds) *The Service-dominant Logic of Marketing: Dialog, Debate and Directions*, pp. 91–104, M. E. Sharp.

Arsel, Z. and Thompson, C.J. (2011) 'Demythologizing consumption practices: how consumers protect their field-dependent identity investments from devaluing marketplace myths', *Journal of Consumer Research* **37** (5), 791–806.

Arbury, A. (2005) *Entertaining Angels*, Sheffield: Sheffield Phoenix Press.

Bagozzi, R.P. (1975) 'Marketing as exchange', *Journal of Marketing* **39** (4), 32.

Bains, P. (2006) *The Primacy of Semiosis: an Ontology of Relations*, Toronto: University of Toronto Press.

Barak, B. and Gould, S. (1985) 'Alternative age measures: a research agenda', *Advances in Consumer Research* **12** (1), 53–58.

Barak, B., Mathur, A., Lee, K. & Zhang, Y. (2001), 'Perceptions of age–identity: A cross-cultural inner-age exploration', *Psychology and Marketing,* **18** (2) 1003-1029.

Barthes, R. (1982) *Empire of Signs*, trans. R. Howard, London: Jonathan Cape.

Bathes, R. (1997) *The Eiffel Tower and other Mythologies*, trans. R. Howard, University of California Press.

Barthes. R. (1999) *The Eiffel Tower & Other Mythologies*, New York: Hill and Wang.

Baudrillard, J. (1993) *Simulacra and Simulation*, trans. S. Farine-Glaser, University of Michigan Press.

Baudrillard, J, (1998) *The Consumer Society: Myths and structures*, London: Sage.

Bauman, Z. (1999) *Culture as Praxis: Theory, Culture and Society*, London: Sage.

BBC (2004) GM 'cow' protest at supermarket, [BBC News Channel], [Online]. Available: http://news.bbc.co.uk/1/hi/wales/3883059.stm [2010, May 10th]

Bekin, C., Carrigan, M. and Szmigin, I. (2005) 'Defying marketing sovereignty: voluntary simplicity at new consumption communities', *Qualitative Market Research* **8** (4), 413–429.

Belk, R.W. (1985) 'Materialism: trait aspects of living in the material world', *Journal of Consumer Research* **12** (3), 265–280.

Belk, R.W. (1993) 'Materialism and the making of the modern American Christmas', in D. Miller (ed.), *Unwrapping Christmas*, Oxford: Clarendon Press, pp. 75–104.

Belk, R.W. (2010) 'Benign envy', Academy of Marketing Conference, available: http://www.youtube.com/watch?v=IZwgznJwGno

Belk, R. W. and Costa, J.A. (1998) 'The mountain man myth: a contemporary consuming fantasy', *Journal of Consumer Research* **25** (3), 218–240.

Belk, R.W., Wallendorf, M. and Sherry, J. (1989) 'The sacred and the profane in consumer behaviour: theodicy on the Odyssey', *Journal of Consumer Research* **16** (June), 1–38.

Bennett, T. (1994) I'm Just a Lucky So and So, in *At Carnegie Hall*, June 9 1962, Sony BMG

Berger, A.A. (2007) *Thailand Tourism*, Haworth Press.

Berlyn, P. (1977) Sacredness & the Environment; Conference proceedings, New ERA Ecumenical Conference, Lisbon June 19-21st 1977

Bernthal, M., Crockett, D. and Rose, R. (2005) 'Credit cards as lifestyle facilitators', *Journal of Consumer Research* **32** (1), 130–145.

Bitner, M.J. (1992) 'Servicescapes: the impact of physical surroundings on customers and employees', *Journal of Marketing* **56** (2), 57–71.

Bitner, M., Faranda, W., Hubbert, A. and Zeithaml, V. (1997) 'Customer contributions and roles in service delivery', *International Journal of Service Industry Management* **8** (3), 193–205.

Bivins, T. (2009) *Mixed Media: Moral Distinctions in Advertising, Public Relations and Journalism*, 2nd edn, New York: Routledge.

Blois, K. (2003) '"Relationships" – a social construction of reality?', *Marketing Thoery* **3** (1), 79–95.

Booms, B.H. and Bitner, M.J. (1981) 'Marketing strategies and organization structures for service firms', in J.H. Donnelly and W.R. George (eds), *Marketing of Services*, American Marketing Association, .

Borden, N.H. (1964) 'The concept of the marketing mix', *Journal of Advertising Research* **4** (2), 7–12.

Botterill, D. (2001) 'The epistemology of a set of tourism studies', *Leisure Studies* **20** (1999), 199–214

Bourdieu, P. (1987) *Distinction: a Social Critique of the Judgement of Taste*, trans. R. Nice, Cambridge, MA: Harvard University Press.

Boyne, R. (2000) 'Post-panopticism', *Economy and Society* **29** (2), 285–307.

Branch, J, (2007) 'Postmodern consumption and the high-fidelity audio microculture, consumer culture theory', *Research in Consumer Behaviour*, **11**, 79-99

Britain Thinks (2011) *A Study of the Middle Classes* available: http://britainthinks. com/sites/default/files/reports/SpeakingMiddleEngish_Report.pdf

Brown, S., Kozinets, R.V. and Sherry, J. (2003) 'Teaching old brands new tricks: retro branding and the revival of brand meaning', *Journal of Marketing* **67** (3), 19–33.

Brown, J., Broderick, A.J. and Lee, N. (2007) 'Word of mouth communication within online communities: conceptualizing the online social network', *Journal of Interactive Marketing* **21** (3), 2–20.

Brown, S., Garino, G., Taylor, K. & Price, S.W. (2005), 'Debt and financial expectations: an individual- and household-level analysis', *Economic inquiry*, **43** (1) 100-120.

Brownlie, D. and Hewer, P. (2007) 'Prime beef cuts: culinary images for thinking "men"', *Consumption Markets and Culture* **10** (3), 229–250.

Brunori, G. (2007) 'Local food and alternative food networks: a communication perspective', *Anthropology of Food*, S3 March.

Brundtland Commission (1987) *Our Common Future*, United Nation

Bryman, A. (2004) *Social Research Methods*, Oxford: OUP.

Burrell, G. and Morgan, G. (1979) *Sociological Paradigms and Organizational Analysis*, Heinemann.

Burt, S. and Sparks, L. (2002) 'Corporate branding, retailing and retail internationalization', *Corporate Reputation Review* **5** (2 & 3), 194–212.

Buttle, F. (1996) 'SERVQUAL: review, critique, research agenda', *European Journal of Marketing* **30** (1), 8–31.

Caillois, R. (1988) *Man and the Sacred*, Glencoe : Free Press.

Carducci, B.J. (2009) *The Psychology of Personality: Viewpoints, Research and Applications*, 2nd Edition, Wiley-Blackwell

Carrigan, M. (1998) 'Segmenting the grey market: the case for fifty-plus lifegroups', *Journal of Marketing Practice: Applied Marketing Science* **4** (2), 43–56

Carrigan, M. and Szmigin, I. (2000) 'Advertising in an ageing society', *Ageing and Society* **20** (2), 217–233.

Carù, A. and Cova, B. (2003) 'Revisiting consumption experience: a more humble but complete view of the concept', *Marketing Theory* **3** (June), 267–286.

Cheong, S. and Miller, M. (2000) 'Power and tourism: a Foucauldian observation', *Annals of Tourism Research* **27** (2), 371–390.

Cherrier, H. (2009), 'Disposal and simple living: exploring the circulation of goods and the development of sacred consumption', *Journal of Consumer Behaviour*, **8** (6) 327-339.

Chronis, A., Arnould, E.J. and Hampton, R.D. (2012) 'Gettysburg re-imagined: the role of narrative imagination in consumption experience', Consumption Markets and Culture, http://www.tandfonline.com/doi/abs/10.1080/10253866.2 011.652823

CIM (2007) 'The good, the bad, and the indifferent – marketing and the triple bottom line, in *Shape the Agenda* issue No.11, 2007

CIM (2010) , *Ethics and Social Responsibility* [Homepage of the Chartered Institute of Marketing], [Online]. Available: http://www.cim.co.uk/resources/ethics/home. aspx [2010, May 10th].

Clark. J. and Critcher. C. (1989) *The Devil Makes Work: Leisure in Capitalist Britain*; London: Macmillan.

Claseen, A. (2007) 'The symbolic function of food as iconic representation of culture and spirituality in Wolfram von Eschenbach' Parzival (ca. 1205)', *Orbis Litteratum* **62** (2), 315–335.

Clegg, S. (1997) *Frameworks of Power*, London: Sage.

Cleland, R.G. (1952), *This Reckless Breed of Men: The Trappers and Fur Traders of the Southwest*, New York: Knopf.

Cockerham, W.C. (2005) 'Health lifestyle theory and the convergence of agency and structure', *Journal of Health and Social Behavior* **46** (1), 51–67.

Cohen, C.B. (1995) Marketing paradise, making nation. *Annals of Tourism Research*, 22(2): 404–421.

Cohen, S. and Taylor, L. (1992) *Escape Attempts: the Theory and Practice of Resistance to Everyday Life*, London: Routledge.

Cole, M. (2008) 'Asceticism and hedonism in research discourses of veg*anism', *British Food Journal*, **110 (7)**, 706 - 716

Cooper, T. 2010) *Longer Lasting Products: Alternatives to the Throwaway Society*, Farnham: Gower.

Couldry, N. (2001) *Inside Culture: Re-imagining the Method of Cultural Studies*. London: Sage.

Cova, B. (1997) 'Community and consumption: towards a definition of the linking value of product of services', *European Journal of Marketing* **31** (3/4), 297–316.

Cova, B. and Cova, V. (2002) 'Tribal marketing: the tribalisation of society and its impact on the conduct of marketing', *European Journal of Marketing* **36** (/6), 595–620.

Cova, B. and Cova, V. (2001) 'Tribal aspects of postmodern consumption: the case of French in-line roller skaters,' *Journal of Consumer Behavior*, **1** (1), 67-76

Cova, B. and Pace, S. (2006) 'Brand community of convenience products: new forms of customer empowerment – the case "my Nutella The Community"', *European Journal of Marketing* **40** (9), 1087–1105.

Crane, A. and Desmond, J. (2002) 'Societal marketing and morality', *European Journal of Marketing* **36** (5/6), 548–569.

Crang, M. (1997) 'Picturing practices: research through the tourist gaze', *Progress in Human Geography* **21** (3), 359–373.

Crick, M. (1989) 'Representations of sun, sex, sights, savings and servility', *International Tourism in the Social Sciences, Annual Review of Anthropology* **18**, 307–344.

Crouch, D. and Desforges, L. (2003) 'The sensuous in the tourist encounter', *Tourist Studies* **3** (1), 5–22.

Culler, J. (1981) 'Semiotics of tourism', *American Journal of Semiotics* **1**, 127–140.

Culler, J. (1988) *Framing the Sign: Criticism and its Institutions*, Oxford: Basil Blackwell.

D'Andrade, R. (1990), 'Cultural Cognition''' in *Foundations of Cognitive Science*, ed. Michael I. Poser, Cambridge, MA: MIT Press, 795–830.

Dann, G. (1996a) 'The people of tourist brochures', in T. Selwyn (ed.), *The Tourist Image: Myths and Myth Making in Tourism*, Chichester: Wiley, pp. 61–82.

Dann, G. (1996b) *The Language of Tourism: A Sociolinguistic Interpretation*, Wallingford: CAB International.

Dabis, F. (1979) *Yearning for Yesterday: a Sociology of Nostalgia*, Glencoe: Free Press.

Davis, J.S. (2005) 'Representing place: deserted islands and the reproduction of Bikini Atoll', *Annals of the Association of American Geographers* **93** (3), 607–625.

Dawkins, N. (2009) 'The hunger for home: nostalgic affect, embodied memories and the sensual politics of transnational foodways'. *UG Journal of Anthropology* **1**, 33–42.

DeCerteau, M. (1984) *The Practice of Everyday Life*, Los Angeles: University of California Press.

Delanty, G. (1997) *Social Science: Beyond Constructivism and Realism*, Buckingham: Open University Press.

Delind, L. (2006) 'Of bodies, places and culture: re-situating local food', *Journal of Agricultural and Environmental Ethics* **19**, 121–146.

Delueze, G. and Guattari, F. (1984) *Nomadology, The War Machine (Semiotext(e)/ Foreign Agents*, MIT Press.

Denny, R.M. and Sunderland, P.L. (2002) 'What is coffee in Bangkok?', *Research Magazine*, Nov., available at http://www.practicagroup.com/pdfs/Denny_and_Sunderland_What_is_Coffee.pdf

Devinney, T., (2010) 'Using market segmentation approaches to understand the green consumer', in *Oxford Handbook of Business and the Environment*, Bansel, P & Hoffman, A (eds) Oxford, 2010.

Drolet, M. (2004) *The Postmodernism Reader: Foundation Texts*, New York: Routledge.

Durkheim. E. (1995) *The Elementary Forms of Religious Life*, London: George Allen and Unwin.

Echtner, C.M. (1999) 'The semiotic paradigm: implications for tourism research', *Tourism Management* **20** (1), 47–57.

Eckhar, G., Belk, B. and Devinney, M. (2010) 'Why don't consumers consume ethically', *Journal of Consumer Behaviour* **9**, 426–436.

Eco U (1990) *Travels in Hyperreality*, trans. W. Weaver, Harcourt Brace & Co.

Eco. U. (1995) *Faith in Fakes: Travels in Hyperreality*, London: Minerva Press.

Eigler, P. and Langeard, E. (1975) 'Une approche novelle pour le marketing des services', *Revue Française de Gestion* **2** (spring), 97–114.

Elkington, J., Hailes, J. and Makower, J. (1990) *The Green Consumer*, New York: Penguin.

Ellis, J. (1980) 'Photography/pornography/art/pornography', *Screen*, **21**, 81–108.

Emanuel, L. (1997) 'An investigation of visitor and resident place perception of mid Wales', in D. Botterill, 'The epistemology of a set of tourism studies', *Leisure Studies* **20** (1999), 214.

Euro RSG. (2010), *Know: The Furure of Travel*, Euro RSCG Worldwide Network.

Fantasia, R. (1995) 'Fast food in France', *Theory and Society* **24**, 201–243.

Featherstone. M. (1991) *Consumer Culture and Postmodernism*, London: Sage.

Ferguson, P. 'A cultural field in the making: gastronomy in 19th century France', *American Journal of Sociology* **104** (3), 597–641.

Ferry, J. (2003) *Food in Film: A Culinary Performance of Communication*, London: Routledge.

Firatt, A.F. and Dholakia, N. (2006) 'Theoretical and philosophical implications of postmodern debates: some challenges to modern marketing', *Marketing Theory* **June** (6), 123–162.

Firat, A.F. and Venkatesh, A. (1995) 'Liberatory postmodernism and the reenchantment of consumption', *Journal of Consumer Research* **22** (3), 239–267.

Firat, A.F., Dholakia, N. and Venkatesh, A. 'Marketing in a post modern world', *European Journal of Marketing*, **29**,1

Fiske, J. (1990) *Introduction to Communication Studies*, 2nd edn, London: Routledge.

Foucault, M. (1980) *Power/Knowledge: Selected Writings and Other Interviews*, New York: Pantheon.

Foucault. M. (1987) *Language, Counter memory, Practice: Selected essays and Interviews*, (Ed Donald Bouchard) Ithaca, Cornell University Press, Boston.

Foucault, M. (2002) *The Archaeology of Knowledge*, Routledge.

Franklin, A. and Crang, M. (2001) 'The trouble with tourism and travel theory', *Tourist Studies* **1** (1), 1–12.

Frow, J. (1991) 'Tourism and the semiotics of nostalgia',MIT Press, October, **57**, 123–151.

Fuat Firat, A. & Dholakia, N. (1998), *Consuming people: from political economy to theaters of consumption*, Routledge.

Gabriel. S. (1993) *The Barbarian Temperament: Towards a Postmodern Critical Theory*, London: Routledge.

Gadamer, G.F. (2004) *Truth and Knowledge*, 2nd edn, London: Continuum Books.

Gadamer, H. (1975) *Truth and Method*, New York: Continuum.

Gaffey, S. (2004) *Signifying Place: the Semiotic Realisation of Place in Irish Product Marketing*, Aldershot: Ashgate.

Gallicano, T. (2011) 'A critical analysis of greenwashing claims', *Public Relations Journal* **5** (3)

Garlick, S. (2002) 'Revealing the unseen: tourism, art and photography', *Cultural Studies* **16** (2), 289–305.

Genosko, G. (2003) 'The bureaucratic beyond: Roger Caillois and the negation of the sacred in Hollywood cinema', *Economy and Society*, **32** (1), 74-89.

Getz, D. and Sailor, M. (1993) 'Design of destination and strraction specific brochures', in U. Musaffer and D. Feisenmainer (eds), *Communication Channel Systems in Tourism Marketing*, New York: Hayworth Press, pp. 191–215.

Giesler, M. (2006) 'Consumer gift systems', *Journal of Consumer Research* **33** (2), 283

Goldsmith, R.E. and Heiens, R.A. (1992) 'Subjective age: a test of five hypotheses', *The Gerontologist* **32** (3), 312–317.

Goulding, C. (1999) 'Heritage, nostalgia and the grey consumer', *Journal of Marketing Practice: Applied Marketing Science* **5** (6/7/8), 177–199.

Goulding, C. (2001) 'Romancing the past: heritage visiting and the nostalgic consumer', *Psychology and Marketing* **18** (6), 565–592.

Goulding, C. and Shankar, A. (2004) 'Age is just a number: rave culture and the cognitively young thirty something', *European Journal of Marketing* **38** (5/6), 641–658.

Goulding, C., Shankar, a., Elliott, R. and Canniford, R. (2009) 'The marketplace management of illicit pleasure', *Journal of Consumer Research* **35** (5), 759–771.

Goulding, G. and Saren, M. (2009) 'Performing identity: an analysis of gender expression at the Whity goth festival', *Consumption Markets and Culture* **12** (1), 27–46.

Graburn, N.H. (1986) 'The anthropology of tourism', *Annals of Tourism Research*, **10**, 530-563.

Grayson, K. and Shulman, D. (2000) 'Indexicality and the verification function of irreplaceable possessions: a semiotic analysis', *Journal of Consumer Research* **27** (1), 17–30.

Grönroos, C. (2008) 'Service logic revisited: who creates value? And who co-creates?', *European Business Review* **20** (4), 298–314.

Grönroos, C. (2011) 'Value co-creation in service logic: a critical analysis', *Marketing Theory* **11** (3), 279–301.

Grove, S. and Fisk, R. (1992) 'The service experience as theater', *Advances in Consumer Research* **19**, 455–461.

Guba, E. and Lincoln, Y. (1989) *Fourth Generation Analysis*, London; Sage.

Gvion, L. and Trostler, N. (2008) 'From spaghetti and meatballs through Hawaiian pizza to sushi: the changing nature of ethnicity in American restaurants', *Journal of Popular Culture* **41** (6), 950–974.

Halewood, C. and Hannam, K. (2001) 'Viking heritage tourism: authenticity and commodification', *Annals of Tourism Research* **28** (3), 565n580.

Hall, S. (1997) *Representation: Cultural representations and Signifying Practices*, Sage.

Hanna, J. (2009), 18th November-last update, *Customer Feedback Not on elBulli's Menu* [Homepage of Harvard Business School Working Knowledge], [Online]. Available: http://hbswk.hbs.edu/item/6105.html [2011, May, Tuesday 10th].

Harvey, D. (1993) 'From space to place and back again: reflections on the condition of postmodernity', in J. Bird, B. Curtis, T. Putnam, G. Robertson and L. Tickner (eds), *Mapping the Futures Local Cultures, Global Change*, London: Routledge, 3–39.

Harvey. D. (1995) *The Condition of Postmodernity*, Oxford: Basil Blackwell.

Hawkes, C. (2009) 'Sales promotions and food consumption', *Nutrition Reviews* **67** (6), 333–342.

Hely, J. (2002) 'Hospitality as sign and Sacrament', *Journal of Religion, Disability and Health* **64** (4), 462–482.

Henry, P. and Caldwell, M. (2008) 'Spinning the proverbial wheel? Social class and marketing', *Marketing Theory* **8** (4), 387–405.

Herbert, D. (1995) 'Heritage as a literary place', in D. Herbert (ed.), *Heritage, Tourism and Society*, London: Mansell, pp. 212–221.

Hickman, M. (2010), Wednesday 19 May-last update, *Online protest drives Nestlé to environmentally friendly palm oil: Food giant bows to Greenpeace campaign and vows to cut its 'deforestation footprint'*. Available: http://www.independent.co.uk/environment/green-living/online-protest-drives-nestl-to-environmentally-friendly-palm-oil-1976443.html [2010, May, 10th].

Hirschman, E.C. (2003) 'Men, dogs, guns, and cars: the semiotics of rugged individualism', *Journal of Advertising* **32** (1), 9–22.

Hodge, R. and Kress, G. (1979) *The Ideology of Language*, Cambridge: Polity Press.

Hodge, R. and Kress, G. (1995) *Social Semiotics*, Cambridge: Polity Press.

Holbrook, M.B. (1993) 'Nostalgia and consumption preferences: some emerging patterns of consumer tastes', *Journal of Consumer Research* **20** (2), 245–256.

Holbrook, M.B. (1996) 'Special session summary: customer value a framework for analysis and research', in K.P. Corfman and J.G. Lynch Jr. (eds) *Advances in Consumer Research*, vol. 23.

Holbrook, M.B. (1999) *Consumer Value: a Framework for Analysis and Research*, London: Routledge.

Hollander, J. (1999) 'Writing of food', *Social Research* **66** (1), 197–211.

Hollinshead, K. (1999) 'Surveillance of the worlds of tourism: Foucault and the eye-of-power', *Tourism Management* **20**, 7–23.

Holt, D.B. (1995) 'How consumers consume: a typology of consumption practices', *Journal of Consumer Research* **22** (1), 1–16.

Holt, D.B. (1997) 'Distinction in America? Recovering Bourdieu's theory of tastes from its critics', *Poetics* **25** (2–3), 93–120.

Holt, D.B. (1998) 'Does cultural capital structure American Consumption', *Journal of Consumer Research* **25** (1), 1–25.

Holt, D.B. (2002) 'Why do brands cause trouble? A dialectical theory of consumer culture and branding', *Journal of Consumer Research* **29** (1), 70–90.

Holt, D.B. (2004a) 'Consumers' cultural differences as local systems of tasters: a critique of the personality/values approach and an alternative framework', in J.A. Cote and S.M. Leong (eds), *Asia Pacific Advances in Consumer Research*, vol. 1, Association for Consumer Research, pp. 178–184.

Holt, D.B. (2004b) *How Brands Become Icons: the Principles of Cultural Branding*, Cambridge, MA: Harvard Business Press.

Holt, D.B. (2006) 'Jack Daniel's America: iconic brands as ideological parasites and proselytizers', *Journal of Consumer Culture* **6** (3), 355–377.

Holt, D.B. and Cameron, D. (2010) *Cultural strategy: Using Innovative Ideologies to Build Breakthrough Brands*, Oxford: Oxford University Press.

Holt, D.B. and Sternthal, B. (1997) 'Poststructuralist lifestyle analysis: conceptualizing the social pattering of consumption', *Journal of Consumer Research* **23** (4), 326–350.

Holt, D. & Thompson, C. (2004), 'Man-of-action heroes: the pursuit of heroic masculinity in everyday consumption', *Journal of Consumer Research,* **31** (2), 425-440.

Hoopes, J. (1991) *Peirce on Signs*, Chapel Hill, NC: University of North Carolina Press.

Hopkins, J. (1998) 'Signs of the post-rural: marketing myths of a symbolic countryside', *Geografiska Annaler* **80** B (2), 65–81.

Houston, F.S. and Gassenheimer, J.B. (1987) 'Marketing and exchange', *Journal of Marketing* **51** (4), 3–18.

Horney, K,. (1945) *Our Inner Conflicts*, New York: Norton & Co.

Howes, D. (2004) *Empire of the Senses: the Sensual Cultural Reader*, London: Berg Publishers.

Hurtado, A. (1993) 'Intimate frontiers: sexual violence and the politics and policies of conquest: Amerindian women and the Spanish conquest of Alta California', in A. de la Torre and B. Pesquera (eds), *Building with Our Hands: New Directions in Chicana Studies*, Berkeley: University of California Press.

Inglis, F. (2000) *The Delicious History of the Holiday*, London: Routledge.

Inskeep, E. (1991) *Tourism Planning: an Integrated Approach*, New York: Van Nostrand Reinhold.

Ireland, M. (1998) 'What is Cornishness? The implications for tourism', *Tourism, Culture and Communication* **1** (1), 17–26.

Izberk-Bilgin, E. (2010) 'An interdisciplinary review of resistance to consumption, some marketing implications, and future research suggestions', *Consumption Market and Culture* **13** (3), 299–323.

Jameson. F. (1985) Postmodernism and Consumer Society; in Foster. H. (Ed) *Postmodern Culture*, London: Pluto.

Jameson, F. (1991) *Postmodernism or the Cultural Logic of Late Capitalism*, London: Verso.

Jenkins, O. (2003) 'Photography and travel brochures: the circle of representation', *Tourism Geographies* **5** (3), 305–328.

Jenkins, R. (2011) 'Consumption in the everyday imagination: how culture gives shape to everyday thinking', PhD thesis, Bournemouth University.

Jin, B., Sternquist, B. and Koh, A. (2003), 'Price as hedonic shopping', *Family and Consumer Sciences Research Journal*, **31**, 378–402

Johns, N. and Pine, R. (2002) 'Consumer behaviour in the food service industry: a review', *Hospitality Management* **21**, 119–134.

Johnson, B. and Thomas, P. (1992) *Choice and Demand in Tourism*, London: Mansell Publishing.

Jokinen, E. and McKie, D. (1997) 'The disorientated tourist: the figuration of the tourist in contemporary cultural critique', in C. Rojek and J. Urry (eds), *Touring Cultures*, London: Routledge.

Jones, P., Comfort, D. and Hillier, D. (2005) 'Corporate social responsibility and the UK's top ten retailers', *International Journal of Retail and Distribution Management* **33** (12), 882–892.

Kahnx, B., Ratner, R., & Kahneman., (1997) 'Patterns of hedonic consumption over time', *Marketing Letters*, **8** (1), 85-96

Kassarjian, H.H. (1971) 'Personality and consumer behaviour: a review', *Journal of Marketing Research* **8** (4), 409–418.

Kates, S. (n.d.) 'Marketing interpretive's communities: a new form of sociocultural segmentation?', working paper.

Kelly, B., Bochynska, K., Kornman, K. and Chapman, K. (2008) 'Internet food marketing on popular children's websites and good product websites in Australia', *Public Health Nutrition* **11** (11), 1180.

Ketchum, C. (2005) 'The essence of cooking shows: how the food network constructs consumer fantasies', *Journal of Communication Inquiry* **29** (3), 217–234.

Klein, H., Hirschheim, R. and Nissen, H. (1991) 'A pluralist perspective of the information research arena', in H. Klein and R. Hirscheim (eds), *Information Research: Contemporary Approaches and Emergent Traditions*, Amsterdam: North Holland.

Kniazeva, M. and Vekatesh, A. (2007) 'Food for thought: a study of food consumption in postmodern US culture', *Journal of Consumer Behaviour* **6** (6), 419–435.

Kotler, P. (1972) 'A generic concept of marketing', *Journal of Marketing* **36** (2), 46–54.

Kotler, P. (2008) *Principles of Marketing*, Harlow: Pearson Education.

Kotler, P. and Levy, S.J. (1969) 'Broadening the concept of marketing', *Journal of Marketing* **33** (1), 10–15.

Kotler, P. and Levy, S.J. (1971) 'Demarketing, yes, demarketing', *Harvard Business Review* **79** (6), 74–80.

Kozinets, R. (2001) 'Utopian enterprise: articulating the meanings of Star Trek's culture of consumption', *Journal of Consumer Research* **28** (1), 67–88.

Kozinets, R.V., Handelman, J.M., & Lee, M.S.W., (2010) 'Don't read this; or, who cares what the hell anti-consumption is, anyways?'. *Consumption Markets & Culture* **13** (3), 225-233.

Kozinets, R., de Valck, K., Wojnicki, A. and Wilner, S. (2010) 'Network narratives: understanding word-of-mouth marketing in online communities', *Journal of Marketing* **74** (2), 71–89.

Kozinets, R.V. (1997) 'I want to believe: a netnography of the X-philes' subculture of consumption', *Advances in Consumer Research* **24** (1), 470n475.

Kozinets, R.V. (1999) 'E-tribalized marketing?: The strategic implications of virtual communities of consumption', *European Management Journal* **17** (3), 252–264.

Kozinets, R.V. (2002a) 'Can consumers escape the market? Emancipatory illuminations from Burning Man', *Journal of Consumer Research* **29** (1), 20–38.

Kozinets, R.V. (2002b) 'The field behind the screen: using netnography for marketing research in online communities', *Journal of Marketing Research* **39** (1), 61–72.

Kozinets, R.V.(2007) ' Inno-tribes: Star Trek as Wikimedia', in B. Cova, R.V. Kozinets and A. Shankar (eds), *Consumer Tribes*, Butterworth-Heinemann, pp. 194–211.

Kozinets, R.V. (2010) *Netnography: Doing Ethnographic Research Online*, London: Sage.

Kozinets, R.V., Iacobucci, D., Mick, D.G., Arnould, E., Sherry, J., John F., Storm, D., Duhachek, A., Nuttavuthisit, K. & DeBerry-Spence, B. (2004) Ludic Agency and Retail Spectacle, *Journal of Consumer Research* **31** (3), pp. 658-672.

Kress, G. and van Leeuwen, T. (1996) *Reading Images: the Grammar of Visual Design*, London: Routledge.

Kress, G. and van Leeuwen, T. (1998) 'Front pages: (the critical) analysis of newschapter layout', in A. Bell and P. Garrett (eds), *Approaches to Media Discourse*, Oxford: Blackwell, pp. 186–219.

Kress, G. and van Leeuwen, T. (2001) *Multimodal Discourse: the Modes and Media of Contemporary Communication*, London: Arnold.

Krippendorf, J. (1999) *The Holiday Makers*, Oxford: Heinemann.

Lages, L. and Fernandes, J. (2005) 'The SERPVAL scale: a multi-item instrument for measuring service personal values', *Journal of Business Research* **58** (11), 1562–1572.

Laing, J.F. (2006) 'Extraordinary journeys: motivations behind frontier travel experiences and implications for tourism', PhD thesis, La Trobe University, Victoria, Australia.

Lane, R. and Waitt, G. (2001) 'Authenticity in tourism and native title: place, time and spatial politics in the East Kimberley', *Social and Cultural Geography* **2** (4), 381- 405.

Lane, R. and Waitt, G. (2007) 'Inalienable places', *Annals of Tourism Research* **34** (1), 105–121.

Lash, S. and Urry, J. (1994) *Economies of Signs and Space*, London: Sage.

Lauterborn, R. (1990) 'New marketing litany: Four Ps Passé: C-Words Take Over.' *Advertising Age* **61**(41), 26.

Law, J. (ed.) (1986) *Power, Action and Belief: A New Sociology of Knowledge*, London: Routledge.

Lefebvre, H. (1991) *The Production of Space*, Oxford: Blackwell.

Levitt, T. (2004) 'Marketing myopia', *Harvard Business Review* **82** (7–8), 138–156.

Levy, S.J. (1959) 'Symbols for sale', *Harvard Business Review* **37** (4), 117–124.

Lofgren, O. (1999) *On Holiday: a History of Vacationing*, London/Berkeley: University of California Press.

Lukes, S. (1974) *Power: A Radical View*, London: Macmillan.

Lusch, R.F. and Vargo, S..L. (2006) *The Service-dominant Logic of Marketing: Dialog, Debate and Directions*, Armonk, NY: M.E. Sharpe.

Lyon, T. and Maxwell, J. (2006) 'Greenwash: corporate environmental disclosure under threat of audit', Ross School of Business Working Paper Series.

Macbeth, J. (2000) 'Utopian tourists – cruising is not just about sailing', *Current Issues in Tourism* **3** (1), 20–34

MacCannell, D. (1999) *The Tourist: A New Theory of the Leisure Class*, Los Angeles: University of California Press.

Magee, R. (2007) 'Food Puritanism and food pornography: the gourmet semiotics of Martha and Nigella', *American Journal of American Popular Culture*, **6** (2)

Maloney, M (1993) 'A personal exploration of critical action research and critical ethnography', Conference Proceedings, Nursing Research Geelong 8th-9th July 1993, Institute of Nursing Research, Deakin University

Marsden, D. & Littler, D. (1998), 'Positioning alternative perspectives of consumer behaviour', *Journal of Marketing Management,* **14** (1-3), 3-28.

Marshall, D. (2005) 'Food as ritual, routine or convention', *Consumption, Markets and Culture*, **8** (1),69–85.

McCabe, D., Rosenbaum, M. and Yurchisin, J. (2007) 'Perceived service quality and shopping motivations: a dynamic relationship', *Services Marketing Quarterly*, **29** (1), 1n21.

McCarthy, J. (1964) *Basic Marketing: A Managerial Approach*, Richard D. Irwin.

McCracken, G. (1986) 'Culture and consumption: a theoretical account of the structure and movement of the cultural meaning of consumer goods', *Journal of Consumer Research* **13** (1), 71–84.

McCracken, G. (1989) 'Who is the celebrity endorser? Cultural foundations of the endorsement process', *Journal of Consumer Research*, **16** (3), 310–321.

McCracken, G. (1993) 'The value of the brand: an anthropological perspective', in D.A. Aaker and A.L. Biel (eds), *Brand Equity and Advertising*, Hillside, NJ: Lawrence Erlbaum Associates, pp. 125–139.

McCracken, G.D. and Roth, V.J. (1989) 'Does clothing have a code? Empirical findings and theoretical implications in the study of clothing as a means of communication', *International Journal of Research in Marketing* **6** (1), 13–33.

McDonald, M. and Dunbar, I. (2010) *Market Segmentation: How to Do It, How to Profit from It*, Oxford: Goodfellow Publishers.

McKuen, R. (1967), *The Gypsey Camp, in the Sea*, Warner Brothers.

Meyrowitz, J. (1992) *No Sense of Place*, New York: Routledge.

Mick, D.G. (1986) 'Consumer Research and semiotics: exploring the morphology of sign, symbols and significance', *Journal of Consumer Research* **13** (2),196–213.

Mick. D.G. and Oswald, L.R. (2006) 'The semiotic paradigm on meaning in the marketplace', in R.W. Belk (ed.) *Handbook of Qualitative Research Methods in Marketing*, Cheltenham: Edward Elgar, pp. 31–45.

Mick, D.G., Burroughs, J.E., Hetzel, P. and Brannen, M.Y. (2004) 'Pursuing the meaning of meaning in the commercial world: an international review of marketing and consumer research founded on semiotics', *Semiotica* **152** (1–4), 1–74.

Middleton, A. (2007) 'Trivialising culture, social conflict and heritage tourism in Quito', International Seminar of Heritage Tourism, CEDLA, Amsterdam, 14–16 June.

Miler, D. (1998), *A Theory of Shopping*, Ithaca, NY: Cornell University Press

Miles, S. (1996) 'The cultural capital of consumption: understanding "postmodern" identities in a cultural context', *Culture and Psychology* **2**, 139–158.

Mintz, S. and Du Bois, C. (2002) 'The anthropology of food and eating', *Annual Review of Anthropology* **31**, 99–119.

Mitchell, I. and Saren, M. (2008) 'The living product n using creative nature of metaphors in the search for sustainable marketing', *Business Strategy and the Environment* **17**, 398–410.

Moisander, J. (2007) 'Motivational complexity of green consumerism', *International Journal of Consumer Studies* **31**, 404–409

Moisander, J. and Pesonen, S. (2002) 'Narratives of sustainable ways of living: constructing the self and other as a green consumer', *Management Decision* **40** (4), 329–342.

Moisander, J. and Valtonen, A. (2006) *Qualitative Marketing Research: A Cultural Approach*, London: Sage.

Morgan, R.M. and Hunt, S.D.(199) 'The commitment–trust theory of relationship marketing', *Journal of Marketing* **58** (3), 20–38.

Morley, D. (2001) 'Belongs: place, space and identity id a mediate world', *Cultural Studies* **4** (4), 425–448.

Mowforth, M. and Munt, P. (1998) *Tourism and Sustainability: New Tourism in the Third World*, London: Routledge.

Nelson, V. (2005) 'Representation and images of people, place and nature in Grenada's tourism', *Geografiska Annaler B* **87** (2), 131–143.

Neto, F. (2002) *Sustainable Tourism, Environmental Protection and Natural Resource Management*, Cancun: UN.

O'Connor, D. (2005) 'Towards a new interpretation of hospitality', *International Journal of Hospitality Management* **17** (3), 267–271.

O'Gorman, K. (2007) 'Dimensions of hospitality: exploring ancient origins', in C. Lashley, P.A. Lynch and a. Morrison (eds), *Hospitality: A Social Lens*, Oxford: Elsevier.

O'Guinn, T.C. and Faber, R.J. (1989) 'Compulsive buying: a phenomenological exploration', *Journal of Consumer Research* **16** (2), 147–157.

O'Shaughnessy, J. and O'Shaughnessy, N.J. (2002) 'Marketing, the consumer society and hedonism', *European Journal of Marketing* **36** (5/6), 524–547.

Oswald, L.R. (2012) *Marketing Semiotics: Signs, Strategies and Brand Value*, Oxford: Oxford University Press.

Panzarella, R. (1980) 'The phenomenology of aesthetic peak experiences', *Journal of Humanistic Psychology* **20** (January), 69–85.

Papworth, J. (2012) 'Money: debt soars as families use plastic to pay bills: borrowing: we owe 48% more than last year as savings drop', *The Guardian*

Parasuraman, A., Zeithaml, V.A. and Berry, L.L. (1988) 'SERVQUAL: a multiple-item scale for measuring consumer perceptions of service quality', *Journal of Retailing* **64** (1), 12–40.

Parsons, P. & Maclaran, P. (2009), *Contemporary Issues in Marketing and Consumer Behaviour*, Taylor & Francis.

Peattie, K. & Peattie, S. (2009), 'Social marketing: A pathway to consumption reduction?', *Journal of Business Research*, **62** (2), 260-268.

Peirce, C.S. (1974) *Collected Chapters: Vols 1, 2, and 5*, eds C. Hartshorne and P. Weiss, Boston, MA: Harvard University Press.

Peñaloza, L. (2000) 'The commodification of the American West: marketers' production of cultural meanings at the trade show', *Journal of Marketing* **64** (4), 82–109.

Peñaloza, L. and Barnhart, M. (2011) 'Living U.S. capitalism, the normalization of credit/debt', *Journal of Consumer Research* **38** (4), 743–762.

Pfaffenberger. B. (1979) 'The Kataragama Pilgrimage: Hindu Buddhist interaction and its significance in Sri Lanka's polyethnic social system', in *Journal of Asian Studies*, **38** (2), 253-70.

Phillimore, J. and Goodson, L. (2004) *Qualitative Research in Tourism: Ontologies, Epistemologies and Methodologies*, London: Routledge.

Picard, M. (1990) 'Cultural tourism in Bali: cultural performances as tourist attraction', *Indonesia* **49** (April), 37–74.

Porter, M.E. (1980) *Competitive Strategy: Techniques for Analyzing Industries and Competitors*, Glencoe:Free Press.

Prahalad, C.K. & Hamel, G. (1990), 'The core competence of the corporation', *Harvard Business Review,* **68** (3), 79-91.

Prayag, G. (2009) 'Tourists' evaluations of destination image, satisfaction and behavioural intentions – the case of Mauritius', *Journal of Travel & Tourism Marketing,* **26** (8), 836-85.3

Price, L.L., Arnould, E.J. and Tierney, P. (1995) 'Going to extremes: managing service encounters and assessing provider performance', *Journal of Marketing* **59** (2), 83

Pritchard, A. and Morgan, N. (2006) 'Hotel Babylon? Exploring hotels as liminal sites of transition and transgression', *Tourism Management* **27** (5), 762–772.

Proctor, T. and Kitchen, P. (2002) 'Communication in postmodern integrated marketing', *Corporate Communications* **7** (3), 144–154.

Randall, S. (1999) 'Television representations of food: a case study of Rick Stein's "Taste of the Sea"', *International Journal of Tourism and Hospitality Research: The Surrey Quarterly,* **1** (1) 41-55.

Rawlins, B. (2009) ' Give the emperor a mirror: toward developing a stakeholder measurement of organizational transparency', *Journal of Public Relations Research* **21** (1), 71–99.

Reed-Danahay, D. (1996) 'Champagne and chocolate: taste and inversion in a French wedding ritual', *American Anthropologist* **98** (4),750–761.

Richardson, B. and Turley, D. (2007) 'It's far more important than that: football fandom and cultural capital', *European Advances in Consumer Research* **8**, 33–38.

Ritzer, G., Dean, P. and Jurgenson, N. (2012) 'The coming of age of the prosumer', *American Behavioral Scientist* **56** (4), 379–398.

Robinson, M. and Andersen, H.C. (eds) (2002) *Literature and Tourism: Essays in the Reading and Writing of Tourism*, London: Thomson.

Rojek, C. (1995) *Decentring Leisure: Rethinking Leisure Theory*, London: Sage

Romero, P. (2008) 'Beware of green marketing, warns Greenpeace exec', ABS-CBN News, available at https://abs-cbnnews.com/special-report/09/16/08/beware-green-marketing-warns-greenpeace-exec

Rook, D.W. (1985) 'The ritual dimension of consumer behavior', *Journal of Consumer Research* **12** (3), 251–264.

Rook, D.W. (1987) 'The buying impulse', *Journal of Consumer Research* **14** (2), 189–199.

Rose, G. (2001) *Visual Methodologies*, London: Sage.

Rubin, L. (ed.) (2008) *Food for Thought: Essays on Eating and Culture*, McFarland & Co Inc

Russell, C.A. and Levy, S.J. (2011) 'The temporal and focal dynamics of volitional reconsumption: a phenomenological investigation of repeated hedonic experiences', *Journal of Consumer Research*, October 28

Said, E. (1995) *Orientalism: Western Conceptions of the Orient*, London: Penguin History.

Saussure, F. (1983) *Courses in General Linguistics*, trans. W. Baskin, London: Duckworth.

Schau, H.J. (2000) 'Consumer imagination, identity and self expression', in S.J. Hoch and R.J. Meyer (eds), *Advances in Consumer Research*, vol. 27, Provo, UT: Association for Consumer Research, pp. 50–56.

Schiffman, L., & Kanuk, L. (2007) *Consumer Behaviour*, 9th Edition, Prentice Hall

Schor, J.B. and Ford, M. (2007) 'From tastes great to cool: children's food marketing and the rise of the symbolic', *Journal of Law, Medicine and Ethics* **35** (1), 10–21

Schroeder, J.E. and Zwick, D. (2004) Mirrors of masculinity: representation and identity in advertising images', *Consumption Markets and Culture* **7** (1), 21–52.

Selwyn. T. (1996) *The Tourist Image: Myths and Myth Making in Tourism*, Wiley, London

Selby, M. (1996) 'Absurdity, phenomenology and place: an existential place marketing project', in Z. Liu and D. Botterill (eds), *Higher Degrees of Pleasure* Proceedings of the International Conference for Graduate Students of Leisure and Tourism, 15th July 1996, UWIC, Cardiff, 49-68

Sered, S. (1988) 'Food and holiness: cooking as a sacred act among Middle-Eastern Jewish women', *Anthropological Quarterly* **61** (3), 129–139.

Sheldrake, P. (2001) *Spaces for the Sacred: Place, Memory and Identity*, Cambridge: SCM Press.

Sheringham, C. and Daruwalla, P. (2007) 'Transgressing hospitality: polarities and disordered relationships?', in C. Lashley, P.A. Lynch and A. Morrison (eds), *Hospitality: A Social Lens*, Oxford: Elsevier.

Sherry, J.F. Jr. (1983) 'Gift giving in anthropological perspective', *Journal of Consumer Research* **10** (2), 157–168.

Sherry, J.F. Jr. (1990) 'Dealers and dealing in a periodic market: informal retailing in ethnographic perspective', *Journal of Retailing* **66** (2), 174–200.

Shore, B. (1996), *Culture in Mind*, New York: Oxford University Press.

Silverstone, R. (1988) 'Television, myth and culture', in J. Carey (ed.) *Media, Myths and Narratives*, Newbury Park, CA: Sage.

Smith, A. (2005) 'Conceptualizing city image change: the "re-imaging" of Barcelona', *Tourism Geographies* **7** (4), 398–423.

Smith, P. (1999) 'Food truck's party hat', *Qualitative Inquiry* **5** (2), 244–261

Solomon, M.R. (1983) 'The role of products as social stimuli: a symbolic interactionism perspective', *Journal of Consumer Research* **10** (3), 319–329.

Solomon, M.R. (2006) *Consumer Behaviour: A European Perspective*, Harlow: Financial Times Prentice Hall.

Solomon, M.R., (2010) *Consumer Behaviour: Buying, Having and Being*, London: Pearson Education.

Solomon, M.R. (forthcoming) *Consumer Behaviour: Buying, Having and Being*, 10th edn, Pearson.

Stirrat. R.L. (1984) 'Sacred Models', *Man* (N.S.) June 1984, **19**, 199-215.

Stoler, A. (2001) 'Tense and tender ties: the politics of comparison in North American history and (post) colonial studies', *Journal of American History* **88** (3), 829–866.

Sturma, M. (1999), 'Packaging Polynesia's image', *Annals of Tourism Research,* **26** (3), 712-715.

Sunderland, P.L. and Denny, R.M.T. (2007) *Doing Anthropology in Consumer Research*, Walnut Creek, CA: Left Coast.

Swarbrook, J. (1998) *Sustainable Tourism Management*, Wallingford: CAB International.

Szmigin, I. and Carrigan, M. (2000) 'Does advertising in the UK need older models?'. *Journal of Product and Brand Management* **9** (2), 128–143.

Szmigin, I. and Carrigan, M. (2001) 'Learning to love the older consumer', *Journal of Consumer Behaviour* **1** (1), 22–34.

Thompson, C. (2004) 'Marketplace mythology and discourses of power', *Journal of Consumer Research* **31** (1), 162–180.

Thompson, C. & Arsel, Z. (2004), 'The Starbucks brandscape and consumers' (anticorporate) experiences of glocalization", *Journal of Consumer Research,* **31** (3), 631-642.

Thompson, C. and Haytko, D. (1997) 'Speaking of fashion: consumers' uses of fashion discourses and the appropriation of countervailing cultural meanings', *Journal of Consumer Research* **24** (June), 15–42.

Thompson, C.J. (1996) 'Caring consumers: gendered consumption meanings and the juggling lifestyle', *Journal of Consumer Research* **22** (4), 388–407.

Thompson, C.J. and Holt, D.B. (2004) 'How do men grab the phallus: gender tourism in everyday consumption', *Journal of Consumer Culture* **4** (3), 313–338.

Thompson, C.J. and Troester, M. (2002) 'Consumer value systems in the age of postmodern fragmentation: the case of the natural health microculture', *Journal of Consumer Research* **28** (4), 550–571.

Thurlow, C. and Aiello, G. (2007) 'National pride, global capital: a social semiotic analysis of transnational visual branding in the airline industry', *Visual Communication* **6** (3), 305–344.

Titscher, S. Meyer, M. *et al.* (2000) *Methods of Text and Discourse Analysis*, London: Sage.

Tresidder, R. (1999) 'Sacred spaces', in D. Crouch (ed.) *Leisure Tourism Geographies: Practices and Geographical Knowledge*, London: Routledge.

Tresidder, R. (2001) 'The representations of sacred spaces in a post-industrial society', in M. Cotter, W. Boyds and J. Gardiner (eds), *Heritage Landscapes: Understanding Place and Communities*, Southern Cross University, pp. 65–76.

Tresidder, R. (2010a) 'What no pasties!? Reading the Cornish tourism brochure', *Journal of Travel and Tourism Marketing* **27** (6), 596–611.

Tresider, R. (2010b) 'Reading food marketing: the semiotics of Marks and Spencer', *International Journal of Sociology and Social Policy* **30** (9/10), 472–485.

Tresidder, R. (2011a) 'Reading hospitality: the semiotics of Le Manoir aux Quat' Saisons', *Hospitality and Society* **1** (1), 67–84.

Tresidder, R. (2011b) 'Health and medical tourism', in P. Robinson, S. Heitmann and P. Dieke (eds), *Research Themes in Tourism*, London: CAB International,

Tucker, H. and Lynch, P.A. (2004) 'Host–guest dating: the potential of improving the customer experience through host–guest psychographic matching', *Journal of Quality Assurance in Hospitality and Tourism* **5** (2/3/4), 11–32.

Tumbat, G. and Belk, R.W. (2011) 'Marketplace tensions in extraordinary experiences', *Journal of Consumer Research* **38** (1), 42–61.

Turner. V. (1973) 'The centre out there: a pilgrim's goal' in *History of Religions*, **12**, 191-230.

Turner, V. (1977) 'Process, performance and pilgrimage: a study', in L.P. Vidyarthi (ed.), *Comparative Symbology*, New Delhi: Concept.

Urry, J. (2001) *The Tourist Gaze: Leisure and Travel in Contemporary Society*, London: TCS.

Uzzell, D. (1984) 'An alternative structuralist approach to the psychology of tourism marketing', *Annals of Tourism Research* **11**, 87–99.

van der Veen, M. (2003) 'When food is a luxury?', *World Archaeology* **34** (3), 405–427

Vargo, S.L. & Lusch, R.F. (2004), 'Evolving to a new dominant logic for marketing', *Journal of Marketing,* **68** (1), 1-17.

Vargo, S.L. and Lusch, R.F. (2008a) 'Service-dominant logic: continuing the evolution', *Journal of the Academy of Marketing Science* **36** (1), 1–10.

Vargo, S.L. and Lusch, R.F. (2008b) 'Why service', *Journal of the Academy of Marketing Science* **36** (1), 25–38.

Veblen, T. ([1899] 2007) *The Theory of the Leisure Class*, Oxford: Oxford University Press.

Waitt, G. and Head, L. (2002) 'Postcards and frontier mythologies: sustaining views of the Kimberley as timeless', *Environment and Planning: Society and Space* **20** (3), 319–344.

Weber. M. (1978) *Selections in Translation,* (Ed. Runciman W.G), Cambridge University Press, Cambridge.

Willets, D. (2011) *The Pinch: How The Baby Boomers Took Their Children's Future - And Why They Should Give It Back,* Atlantic Books

Wlliams, A. (2006) 'Tourism and hospitality marketing: fantasy, feeling and fun', *International Journal of Contemporary Hospitality Management* **18** (6), 482–495.

Wind, Y. (1978) 'Issues and advances in segmentation research', *Journal of Marketing Research* **15** (3), 317–337.

Winstead, K.F. (2000) 'Service behaviors that lead to satisfied customers', *European Journal of Marketing* **34** (3/4), 399–417.

Wool, Z. (2011) 'Aldi effect is back: spending squeeze lifts discounter into profit again: German chain's sales up 25% in last quarter; Tesco losing market share after difficult six months', *The Guardian*, October 4.

Young, M. (1999) 'The relationship between place meanings and tourist motivation', *Tourism Geographies* **1**, 35–60.

York, M. (2001) 'New Age commodification and appropriation of spirituality', *Journal of Contemporary Religion* **6** (3), 12–27.

Zeithaml, V., Parasuraman, A. and Berry, L. (1990) *Delivering Quality Service: Balancing Customer Perceptions and Expectations,* New York: Free Press.